THE BRIDGE BETWEEN US

Becoming One in Marriage

To: Mrs Ruby → The Lord bless
and Keep you.

Dr. Rick D. Merritt

ISBN 978-1-0980-9273-3 (paperback)
ISBN 978-1-0980-9274-0 (digital)

Christian Faith Publishing, Inc.
832 Park Avenue
Meadville, PA 16335
www.christianfaithpublishing.com

ESV
KJV
NIV
MERRIAM-WEBSTER

Printed in the United States of America

I would like to dedicate this book to my wife, Judith, for her loving patience and constant companionship in this process. Your encouragement has meant more than you will ever know. You are without doubt the wind beneath my wings.

CONTENTS

ACKNOWLEDGMENTS

I would like to thank all of my friends who encouraged me to write this book and didn't allow me to hide behind fear and laziness.

FOREWORD

"The Bridge Between Us" by Rick Merritt combines many years of education, innumerable hours of prayerful counseling of countless couples and individuals, personal and pastoral experience together with wisdom and insight given by God to produce a short but powerful and practical book offering real help for all Christians in interpersonal relationships, especially marriage.

Rick Merritt uses 'bridges' to define and expertly examine the gulfs, and sometime chasms, between people; why they exist and how to 'bridge' those gaps of understanding, personality, and maturity. "The Bridges Between Us" cuts through the fog of endless personal counseling with clear, practical, 'to the point' understanding of the things that separate people in relationship. He gives practical, but spiritual, Biblical solutions to bridging gaps that seem so difficult and threaten the survival or marriages

This book is obviously written out of a heart that yearns to see love and unity in every home and family. I believe it will go a long way toward accomplishing that. I would certainly recommend this title to any couple's ministry or small groups focusing on marriage. Many of the principles in the book will also help individuals to understand the obstacles and difficulties that they have in all relationships with other people.

I love that all of the problems and the solutions find their genesis and their power in God and His word. Ecclesiastes 4:12 says, *"Though one may be overpowered by another, two can withstand him. And a threefold cord is not quickly broken."* In this book the author provides real help to those who understand the need for God to be intimately involved in their marriage.

Don Schulze, D.Min.
Pastor of Voyage Church, Flagler Beach, Fl
and author of "A Life of Miracles",
Tydale/Momentum 2014

The Bible declares, *"there is no new thing under the sun"*, but Dr. Merritt's work in "The Bridge Between Us" is as fresh and inspirational as anything I have read on the marriage relationship in over four decades of pastoral ministry. As a pastor reading through the book, I was inspired by the skillful blending of scripture and practical illustration and often found myself thinking, *"that'll preach!"* As a husband of 49 years, I was deeply moved on a personal level and thought more than once, *"I needed this"*. This is not a book to be read and relegated to a bookshelf, but a book to be referenced often for insight, guidance and help.

Pastor Gregory V. Johnson

Why Bridges?

Many excellent books have been written about marriage over the years, and this book is not intended to take their place. Many books have also been written about the differences between men and women. What I intend to do with this short book is focus instead on the commonalities between men and women, husbands and wives.

In an effort to showcase the similarities between men and women, I've chosen the metaphor of bridges, which I will carry throughout this book. I've also included a "bridging the gap" section at the end of each chapter for use in premarital or marital counseling—or even for couples reading through this book themselves.

So take a walk with me into the world of solution-based thinking about the strengths, struggles, and snares of marriage. I know that not all marriages have the same challenges, mainly because every marriage consists of two different people from different backgrounds.

Most of us have read or heard about the differences between men and women, and how distinct we are in our perspectives on life issues. Those differences are real and are meant to complement each other for the purposes of fulfilling our designed destinies. God created man and woman in his image with the purpose of having them coming together *in their uniqueness* to rule his creation. Marriage is the first covenant relationship that combines the whole of two to walk as one.

Though man is uniquely designed for his role as man, and woman is uniquely designed for her role as woman, they are also uniquely compatible for marriage to fulfill God's plan for humanity. God knew the man's biological makeup and the woman's biological makeup would also complement their psychological differences. God had marriage in mind from the beginning as his plan for creation. From the Old Testament to the New Testament, marriage is the vehicle used to promote God's plan of redemption. The gospel starts with a marriage in Eden, and it all ends with a marriage feast in heaven. This is the cause of Satan's hatred toward humanity, which constitutes the mockery and the demonic assault on marriage today.

Marriage is where man and woman are designed to become one, and find their highest expression of worship in marriage through the becoming-one process.

If you're single and happen to be reading this book, it doesn't mean that you're unable to offer God the highest worship you can in your singleness. Your life should be focused on growing in the knowledge and the grace of Christ Jesus (2 Peter 3:17–18), which will prepare you for marriage if it's in your future.

God knew what our differences would be when he created us, yet he designed us to come together and fulfill one another. God created man (Adam), then took a rib from Adam, and created woman (Eve). We who believe the Bible must get our wisdom for understanding our spouse from that truth. Adam and Eve—husband and wife—is the perfect plan out of God's word. Yet our society has created a culture of identity for women and men that have nothing to do with God's original design for the woman or the man. Thus, the reason we have terms such as "toxic masculinity," which is meant to demean the original purpose of God's plan for the man to lead and be the head of the marriage. The aggressive agenda of confusing the gender and mudding the lines of boy and girl distorts the simple truth that God created them—male and female—in his image. I could go further in this discussion, but it would only take away from the direct approach in this book to address godly relationships on a biblical perspective.

We are more in common than we are different for many reasons. For instance, in our relationships,

- we are created for fellowship with God (1 Corinthians 1:9) and companionship with humanity (Ecclesiastes 4:9–10);
- we all need to be affirmed of our self-worth (Luke 12:6–7);
- we all want to be acknowledged and respected (Matthew 7:12, 1 Peter 2:7);
- we all want to feel loved and cherished (1 John 4:11); and

- we all want our individualism celebrated and appreciated, not condemned or suffocated (Romans 12:4–8).

Those are emotional needs that exist in men and women.

A word about bridges

In the history of the world, many negotiations have been won or lost on bridges. Bridges represent the point of transition, crossover, and advancement. They are vital for providing much-needed supplies to sustain strength and progress. They are also points of barriers to keep the enemy out of the borders of home territory. Victory can be won or lost determined by what takes place at the bridge.

Before the invention of the bridge, there was very limited progress for connecting civilizations. You've probably heard the idiom "All roads lead to Rome." Rome was the first ancient empire to perfect bridge building; ancient Roman engineers found that ground volcanic rocks could serve as an excellent material for making mortar. This invention enabled them to build more effective, sturdier, powerful, and larger structures than were constructed in Mesopotamia or any other civilization before them. Seeing the power of roads and connections to distant lands, Roman architects soon spread across Europe, Africa, and Asia, building bridges and roads of very high quality. Because of it, they were able to conquer and command other civilizations.

Bridges serve as the perfect reference as a visual and practical application of how important it is to have connectivity in our marriage relationship. The bridge represents the point of communication, the place of encounter, for the sake of expressing ourselves the best we know how—particularly on issues where we have disagreements or where we find ourselves challenged trying to understand a different viewpoint.

Marriage is a bridge-building process from the moment we say "I do." In fact, we should have begun the bridge-building process before we got married. We should possess the tools for honest, respectful, and open communication before we are standing at the altar on the wedding day. This book will give you these tools throughout each chapter.

A word about differences

While this book will be mostly about our similarities and how to bridge the gap between one another, I do think it's important to acknowledge the differences between men and women here before we move on.

Nothing up to this point is meant to dismiss the psychological differences between men and women. In 1 Peter 3:7, God tells the husband to consider the wife as the weaker vessel, which has nothing to do with the woman's created purpose. She is complete in her design perfectly to be a helper to man. The woman is considered vulnerable only in marriage through the spiritual battle she fights to remain in submission to an imperfect husband. Though the Bible doesn't give us much information to the emotional and psychological warfare of her disposed position as a wife in warfare, trust me, the enemy is seeking every opportunity to unravel her confidence and worth in marriage. Though she is designed to follow, she is also designed to lead. This is where some marriages break down or struggle to maintain divine order according to God's will. In marriage, the woman is not required to give up her authority as a wife. She is required only to submit her authority, meaning, bring her authority under the leadership of her husband. Why?

Though her physical design may appear weaker, Scripture is revealing the power of unity in marriage. When the husband is not in a place of covering his wife with his actions and his words, the enemy has access to her spiritually, which will expose every emotional and psychological weakness that exists in her, which will in turn promote a spiritual weakness.

The same importance is for wives in understanding their role to strengthen the marriage by corroborating with their husbands to preserve their ego as men. When we consider one another as individuals who deserve Christian virtue bestowed on them as we do to others, we're acknowledging our need for that same consideration.

A word about similarities

Though there are obviously gender nuances in the way God has designed man and woman for their ultimate expression in his will, the fact remains: God is not the author of chaos or confusion.

I've heard men say, "Women are just difficult, and you can never really understand them." The criteria used to establish or substantiate that statement often comes from a biased or androcentric (man-centric) philosophy of women. In other words, husbands who say that have not put forth enough effort to work with or understand the idiosyncrasies of their wives. It's a lazy declaration at best, if not an entirely ignorant one. Husband, the next time you feel the urge to voice that statement, remember God created your wife, and God is not the creator or author of confusion.

I've also heard women resigned to the belief that men are nothing more than selfish and lazy creatures of lust. It's true that men are visual creatures by design. A man is meant to see a woman and say, "Whoa! Do you have plans to be happy for the rest of your life, because I'd like to help you with that!" A godly man gives the very thing that his wife craves from him: attention. A godly man sees his wife as the only object of his affection and desires; he chases her, to make dreams come true for her. He's happiest when his wife makes him feel like he can do anything for her.

God has designed the husband to thrive under the influence of his wife's love. And he has designed the wife to thrive through the attention of her husband. They will both thrive in the relationship, reaching their fullest potential through partnership and equal expression in making the marriage successful.

CHAPTER 1

Building Sound Bridges

Soundness /ˈsoun(d)nəs/: the ability to withstand force or stress without being distorted, dislodged, or damaged.

On March 4, 1887, three hundred people boarded a commuter train in Boston. Just after seven in the morning, full of people headed to work and school, the train started crossing the Bussey Bridge. With the train fully on the bridge, the bridge collapsed, killing thirty-seven people and injuring forty others.[1]

Upon inspection, the City of Boston found that the bridge had not been built strong enough to withstand the load. Some pieces that were integral to the soundness of the bridge had rusted through, and the accident was deemed preventable.

This sad story reminds us that our relationships need to be built well with the correct pieces in order to be sound enough to hold the weight of marriage. I can't emphasize

---

[1] http://www.celebrateboston.com/disasters/bussey-bridge-wreck.htm, accessed December 10, 2018

strongly enough that we need to constantly pursue sound-ness in our marriage. It will be a lifelong project.

The Bible tells us in Psalm 139:14 that we are "fearfully and wonderfully made." This is the work of perfection by the hand of God. In the same way, in our marriages, we are to pursue wholeness through Jesus independently of fears, failures, physical imperfection, and the lack of a perfect childhood.

Marriage is meant to strengthen, enhance, and create a sense of sanctuary in your life; God never meant our marriages to be a place of codependency where weaknesses are made vulnerable, and insecurities are abused. (In our fallen world, though, marriage is not two perfect people doing everything right; rather, it is two flawed people learning to walk in their vulnerabilities, and to trust each other.)

Building this kind of marriage is not for the faint of heart and is not a fairy tale. Marriage requires adjustments, the kind that challenges your independence and forces you to surrender entitlements. You must always be considering your spouse (i.e., Will my behavior affect my spouse and my marriage in a negative or positive way?).

Building your side of the bridge

In the process of two people becoming one in marriage, we need to focus first on the individual. Who we are as individuals is who we bring into our relationships. What do you bring to the relationship?

The man and the woman cannot walk in their roles as husband and wife until both are individually submitted to the lordship of Jesus. "I've noticed that the churches with the healthiest married couples promote soundness as individuals, not just soundness as couples."

Here are some questions you can ask yourself concerning your personal quest to soundness:

- Do I need the approval of others to maintain focus and committed to my goals?
- Do I make excuses for others when they mistreat or disrespect me?
- Do I get depressed or angry when others don't take my advice?
- Do I have a hard time saying no even if I know I should?
- Do I lie or compromise my integrity just to keep me in a good light?

These questions can be asked to reveal other vices outside of relationships, but put them in the context of your present relationships, and where do you find yourself? If the answer to any of these is yes, the rest of this chapter is for you.

Personal emotional triggers (PETs)

We all come into our marriage with personal emotional triggers (PETs). These are the hidden issues of the heart that we try to keep out of sight. Most times, we have done such a great job of hiding them that we don't even remember that they are there until we allow someone to get close enough to us to trigger our deepest secrets and insecurities; then the "wall of defenses" goes up, and our spouse becomes our opponent without warning. We think things like, "Why do I feel like they're deliberately trying to pick a fight?" and "How can I be so misunderstood?" It's after such encounters, and our confidence has been shaken, that we feel alone and abandoned, in some cases betrayed by the very ones that we trust most.

What has happened is you've been triggered in one of the hidden places in your emotional psyche. Life is full of opportunities, especially in marriage, that will require our hidden self to come to the surface. We often carry buried offenses and pain from our youth that has in some way shaped our psychological disposition. Sometimes, these offenses and pains include words spoken in anger, intentional acts of hatred, betrayal, and rejection from those you love and respect. It could be past physical and emotional abuse that often get pushed down into the cellar of our active life, or in the background of our lives, to escape shame and guilt.

I believe there are three tools we must possess to build soundness in our marriages, bring our best person forward, and overcome our PETs. We'll start with what we believe, move on to what we think, and end with what we do.

A relationship with Jesus Christ. Coming to a saving knowledge of salvation through Jesus is the key. Asking God to forgive you of your sins and make Jesus your Lord and Savior, forsaking your old life and living for Jesus needs to happen first. Your marriage must have him as the foundation, and God's Word as the glue that holds it together. Too many couples struggle unnecessarily looking for happiness through their spouse when they should be cultivating a deeper commitment to Jesus. We cannot bring spiritually to our marriage what we do not possess. It is the strength, or the lack thereof, of our personal relationship with Jesus that will sustain and ground us.

Marriage is a covenant relationship that should hold a higher standard of respect and openness than we have with common acquaintances. Often the marriage relationship is where we abandon our carnal restraints in thought, speech, and actions. But it should be the place where our Christlike behavior is most displayed. Every attribute that is honed by a surrendered heart to produce godliness is tested in our closest relationships. Marriage is a spiritual yet practical bond of hearts pursuing the will of the Father as individuals, yet united. Not until we desire to please God will we acknowledge the need to address our behavior that displeases him.

When you have a relationship with Jesus, you learn to love his Word, the Bible. I speak with couples all the time who use God's Word to correct their spouses without allowing that same Word to govern their own behavior. The challenges of marriage will demand from you what you don't expect; it will require from you selflessness you may not have cultivated. Your relationship with God will become the source of your conduct in marriage. In your personal worship of Jesus, you learn to challenge our carnal mind with God's Word.

In the age of Google, it is easier to research for philosophical and worldly answers instead of reading God's Word and praying for God's heart on a matter. The Word must first be ingested in our spirit in order for it to have an expression in our behavior. I believe to many Christians today have an emotional relationship with the Word of God, not a converted life relationship. If that is the case, the Word of God does not have root in us; we are not trusting in the Word to guide us or govern our behavior.

Healthy Christian marriages rely on biblical influence as the absolute reference of truth and help in their marriages. As I mentioned, if the foundation is not the Word of God, there will be no strength of God in their practical application of working through life issues.

What we believe (the Gospel of Jesus) determines how we should think, and that brings us to our next sound-bridge-building tool:

Mastery of our thoughts. Our mind is the storehouse for all kinds of perceptions, real or false. There are memories from our past that we bring with us into all relationships. We must deal with the issues of our mind in order to function honestly and allow trust to flourish.

Author James Allen observed: "We do not attract that which we *want* but that which we *are*." The harsh reality is this; we have the harvest that we've sown.

Similarly, in the Bible, we read:

> For as a man thinketh in his heart, so is he. (Proverbs 23:7)

> Finally brethren, whatsoever things are true, whatsoever things are honest, whatsoever things are just, whatso-

ever things are pure, whatsoever things
are lovely, whatsoever things are of good
report; if there be any virtue, and if there
be any praise, think on these things.
(Philippians 4:8)

In Dr. Daniel G. Amen's book *Change Your Brain,
Change Your Life*, he highlights what he calls the 18/40/60
rule to help his clients overcome obsession of worrying
about what others think of you. The rule goes like this:

- When you're eighteen, you worry about what
  everyone is thinking of you.
- When you're forty, you don't give a hoot about
  what anybody thinks of you.
- When you're sixty, you realize nobody's been thinking about you at all.

He states that the energy you put into worrying about
what others think of you is a total waste. That it is energy
they could constructively put into meeting personal goals.

The struggle is to break emotional ruts that shape our
thought process. When we have been conditioned by words
and actions into certain thought patterns from our youth, we
don't change over time just because we get older. We must
deliberately discipline our thoughts to break those patterns.

We can identify these unhealthy patterns by identify-
ing our PETs; they have much to do with the way we protect ourselves because of past pain and disappointments in
life. For instance, we may struggle to overcome familiar

insecurities; our thinking and unhealthy behavior patterns may have come from past words and deeds from others—or ourselves. Sometimes the structure of the homes we grew up in can create PETs that we're not aware of until someone who didn't grow up in that same environment opposes our thinking or behavior.

It doesn't matter how big or small the issue is; it could be anything from finances or sex, to where you keep your toothbrush or if you take your shoes off in the house. When you are triggered by your spouse's behavior, you initially feel shock and/or betrayal. Your mind may immediately jump to, "My spouse doesn't understand me the way I need him/her to." Depending on how we've been taught to process disappointment, we may feel the need to defend our individuality. The enemy is very good at capitalizing on these moments by making us view our spouse as an opponent instead of a partner.

Instead of giving in to those thoughts, we must renew our minds in Christ; take out the trash that clutter and pollute us in our thoughts and emotions. The only way to renew our mind is to be different in the moment. Change your mind, change your outcome. Christ is our mentor into all things promoting grace into us, and into our marriage. Let him lead you when prompted to be gracious.

I'm not denying that this process can take a long time. These moments when we're thinking wrongly about ourselves and our spouses require openness and sensitivity on both parts to overcome and establish trust, which brings us to the next sound-bridge-building tool:

Honesty about our pain. To identify what is the cause of our pain is to acknowledge where we need healing. Notice I said healing, not fixing. Healing a whole concept of our mind body and soul touched by the hand of God to empower us out of weakness. Fixing is elevating our frustrations by changing our circumstance without changing us. Until you're able to be honest about your pain, you're going to rely on someone or something to fix external frustrations, when the problem is really internal. We can only be triggered by what is already present inside of us: offenses, insecurities, rejections, fear, pride, etc.

Psalm 73:21 says, "Thus my heart was grieved, and I was vexed in my mind." This psalmist sums up a disposition of heart that is too often the truth about how we really feel on the inside. We suppress our pain, thinking ignoring it will make it go away, only to be carried away in a sudden rush of emotions when triggered, no matter how hard we try to be different in the moment.

This is called "familiarity recall"; you're reliving a memory of pain. Most couples never take a moment to assess where the pain is really coming from. They blame each other and make demands that have nothing to do with the real problem. (All of this is nothing more than the strategy of the enemy to keep each other in your own personal hurt lockers, by the way. If the enemy can keep us separated and untrusting in our relationship, we will remain alone in our pain.)

Our insecurities and fears have taught us to hide in plain sight, yet we try to function as if nothing is wrong. Somewhat like a functioning alcoholic or drug addict, we know we're under the influence of something, but we'll never admit it. It's possible you have experienced negative outcomes in the past when you have tested the waters with someone you thought would understand, just to be disappointed when you exposed your true feelings. Maybe marriage for you is (or already has been) just another environment where you can be abused, rejected, blamed, or abandoned. Healing will start taking place when you are honest in the deepest part of your heart. Read what the psalmist says here:

> Behold, you delight in truth in the
> inward being, and you teach me wisdom
> in the secret heart. (Psalm 51:6)

God waits for us to admit what he already knows: we hurt and don't know how to be honest and trust in relationship with the frustration of our pain. As the saying goes, "Hurt people hurt people," so we react to the trigger instead of respond to the situation.

What is the difference between reacting and responding? Think of it this way. "Reacting" is an individual or singular action that's all about me, whereas "responding" is a partnership to control the outcome of any incident.

Here's an illustration that might help us understand: Let's say I have a broken toe. I inform you that I broke my toe yesterday, which is why I'm only wearing sandals and walking funny. Not even a minute later, you scoot back your chair—straight into my broken toe. I react strongly. I shout, I push the chair, and I scream at you, "Why did you

DO that? I JUST told you my toe is broken!" Tears stream down my cheeks, and I hop around for a few minutes, because I somehow think that will help.

Now let's say the same thing happens: I tell you about my broken toe, and you accidentally back your chair up into it. Instead of reacting toward you, I instead scream "ouch," hop around a bit, and sit down and try to hold back tears. When the pain subsides a bit, I say, "Maybe you can put your chair where you want it now, and I can just stay here for a few minutes." I forgive you for unintended pain, and we work toward a solution to avoid that situation again anytime soon.

Do you see the difference between reaction and response? I may not be able to avoid the pain you've caused me, but I have a choice of whether to lash out or work through the problem.

When we're honest about our existing pain, it opens us up to searching for solutions. The Word of God is the healing agent that penetrates the secret areas of our lives. Until we allow God's Word to infiltrate these secret places, until we learn to control our thoughts, we will continue to hide our pain in plain sight, unable to bring it into the light and address it honestly.

Reflection questions:

1. What area of our relationship do I struggle to be in partnership with my spouse?
2. Am I aware of my PETs, and do they misrepresent me?
3. Am I keeping my relationship with Jesus vibrant?

CHAPTER 2

The Bridge of Hope

Why bridges? Because they can be used to bring things together, or keep things apart. The bridge connects our lives in many ways on a daily basis without even considering why we think or act the way we do.

The primary reason that bridges are needed in marriage is for the same reason they're needed in life—to join two sides together that would otherwise remain separated. Marriage is a union of two different personalities with different ideas about different things. Bridges symbolize the venue for compromises where agreements can be reached while respecting and honoring one another in marriage.

Covenant versus contract

God established marriage as a covenant, not a contract (Malachi 2:14; Proverbs 2:16–17). Three important differences exist between the two:

Covenant	Contract
Based on yielded trust between parties	Based on voided distrust
Based on unlimited responsibility	Based on limited liability
Cannot be broken if new circumstances occur	Can be voided by mutual consent

The marriage covenant between a man and a woman is a comprehensive and permanent commitment. This was ordained by God for two reasons:

1. Because God is faithful. Marriage is meant to be a picture of Christ's unfailing love and faithful relationship to his church (Ephesians 5:22–33; Revelation 21:2, 9).
2. Because people are fickle. There are few life situations that test true Christianity more than the intimacy of the marriage relationship. Due to the close nature of the marriage relationship, sins of selfishness, pride, laziness, and impatience are readily exposed on a daily basis. The apostle Paul vividly describes our natural tendencies in 2 Timothy

3:1–13 when he describes us as selfish, arrogant, and unloving.

Our sinful tendencies are superimposed on the marriage relationship, thus testing Christian character in the areas of sacrificial love, respect, submission, forgiveness, and perseverance. Even in our sinfulness, though, we can rejoice that Jesus came—not just to put up with our fickleness, not just to counsel it a little and make the best of a bad situation, but to completely remove it so that we can walk in newness of life. In that newness of life, we can repent, reconcile, and forgive—thus living out the Gospel of Jesus daily, constantly, and consistently.

As much as we would all love for our marriages to be conflict-free, that rarely happens. When conflict arises, how do we dwell together in unity (Psalm 133:1) in our covenant relationship? We embrace biblical means of resolving conflict and demonstrating Christian love. Both husbands and wives must pursue love as defined in Ephesians 5:25–30—a sacrificial, purifying, and steadfast love.

Ways to do that is by taking time to listen to one another. The wife wants to be listened to with consideration of her perspective, and the husband wants to be heard with consideration of his perspective. Understand, this is an expression of love to the wife, for her thoughts to be valued and made important. This is also an expression of respect for the husband, to not have his thoughts challenged at every turn because they are not like yours, wife.

The primary purpose of marriage

In the letter to the Ephesians, Paul gives us one of the most instructive passages on marriage in the whole Bible. Let's read it now:

> Wives, submit yourselves unto your own husbands, as unto the Lord. For the husband is the head of the wife, even as Christ is the head of the church: and he is the saviour of the body. Therefore as the church is subject unto Christ, so let the wives be to their own husbands in everything. Husbands, love your wives, even as Christ also loved the church, and gave himself for it; That he might sanctify and cleanse it with the washing of water by the word, That he might present it to himself a glorious church, not having spot, or wrinkle, or any such thing; but that it should be holy and without blemish. So ought men to love their wives as their own bodies. He that loveth his wife loveth himself. For no man ever yet hated his own flesh; but nourisheth and cherisheth it, even as the Lord the church: For we are members of his body, of his flesh, and of his bones. For this cause shall a man leave his father and mother, and shall be joined unto his wife, and they two shall be one flesh. (Ephesians 5:22–31)

In verse 26, God talks about "the washing of the water of the word." This is a direct admonishment given to husbands; use the Word to sanctify and cleanse for the sake of covering your wife. Wives need to be careful that they do not become an instrument of discouragement with their words when they speak to and over their husbands.

Meaning, wives, the words you choose can build your husband up or tear him down in his efforts to lead. You should ask yourself, How would Jesus speak to my husband?

The apostle Peter speaks in clearer terms when he challenges both husband and wife to portray Christlike conduct. (My take is, anything Jesus speaks to the church should also be first exampled in the home, particularly the marriage.)

> Finally, be ye all of one mind, having compassion one of another, love as brethren, be pitiful, be courteous: Not rendering evil for evil, or railing for railing: but contrariwise blessing; knowing that ye are thereunto called, that ye should inherit a blessing. For he that will love life, and see good days, let him refrain his tongue from evil, and his lips that they speak no guile: Let him eschew evil, and do good; let him seek peace, and ensue it. (1 Peter 3:8–11)

If we simply take a moment to pause and take a moment before we speak, it would allow the Holy Spirit to put us in check. I'm not talking about putting on a spiritual facade in the midst of a heated moment by demanding that the two of you should pray. Praying with an entitled mind that you're right and that your spouse needs fixing is not praying. May I take a moment to also say that Scripture is not supposed to be used to condemn one another. Husband or wife is holding stones engraved with scriptures that entitle them to execute judgement without first examining their own hearts with that same word. By the time they are setting in front of me, both have collected a bag of stones to justify their anger or contempt.

Listening is a discipline that is so needed in relationships but often gets overrun by the spirit of contention and pride in our relationships. How can we respond effectively to the real issues of our spouse's heart's cry in conversation if we don't engage our heart as well as our ears?

How often have you tried to explain something in your heart, but words got in the way? A wise spouse will listen to your heart—not only the words that have been spoken. Pain often speaks louder than words when communicating, if we only listen. The enemy wants us to hear pain as an argument or a challenge to defend ourselves. So if we're in an argumentative disposition while in conversations with our spouse, we're unable to be an effective listener, teacher, or student in the moment. Be on guard to keep our hearts open even in challenging conversations.

They are not of the world, even as I am not of the world. Sanctify them through thy truth: thy word is truth. (John 17:16–17)

King David said in Psalm 119:105, "Thy word is a lamp unto my feet, and a light unto my path," and in verse 11, "Thy word have I hid in mine heart, that I might not sin against thee."

God has always had an ordained plan for marriage from the beginning; it is to be the first physical expression and picture of his love for man and woman in the union of fulfilled happiness. Even though God had created for six days and said it was good, it wasn't till he created man, then he said it was very good. Let's look at the first thing God says about marriage in the Bible:

> For this reason a man shall leave his father and his mother, and be joined to his wife; and they shall become one flesh. (Genesis 2:24)

He is saying here that marriage is the expression and the means by which married couples demonstrate their love for God, in their love for each other.

Douglas Wilson states:

> The wedding ceremony is not an end in itself. In fact, marriage is not an end in itself. Marriage is a means of serving and glorifying God. Young women who view marriage as their chief goal are turning the wedding and the married state into an idol.

God planned for marriage to be a blessed state of mutual service to him.

Marriage is not meant to eliminate all of our personal hurts and insecurities. On the contrary, it can easily exacerbate any hidden issues.

The way to avoid the trap of making your marriage an idol is focusing on your personal growth in Christ. God is the one who makes our marriage a place of fulfillment, so we strive to make him our motivation in placing our spouse. When couples have the wrong motivations in marriage, it sets them up for failed expectations and isolated individualism in marriage. The couple that nurtures their personal relationship with Jesus will have a healthy approach in becoming one in marriage, bringing glory to God in their shared goals.

It's possible to be in love with the concept of marriage and not be in love with the person you're married to.

I've sat in front of couples that are trying so hard to be happy in their marriage, working very hard at doing everything in their power to please their spouses, and be the best partners they can be in marriage. On the surface, this sounds very admirable, but in talking to these husbands and wives, I've discovered that they have an image in their minds that has become an idol that they worship and give their allegiance to. The perfect marriage, for some people, is an idol that takes the place of God.

In making marriage an idol, we elevate our image of marriage to an unhealthy place, comparing all things good or bad to that image. This is a common trap for well-meaning Christians in marriage; the desire to be happy becomes paramount, taking precedence over the lordship of Jesus. He is the one who provides all sufficiency to every area of our life and our marriage. Our spouse was never designed to meet every need in our life in companionship, enjoyment, or fruitfulness.

Secondary purposes of marriage

Once husband and wife embrace God's primary purpose for marriage, they will encounter numerous secondary purposes or blessings of a Christ-honoring relationship. Many couples have the tendency to pursue these secondary purposes over God's primary purpose. While secondary purposes are good and worthy of pursuit, they should be viewed as blessings resulting from God's primary purpose for marriage—that of modeling Christ's love for his church through the development of Christian character.

Secondary purposes for marriage could include:

1. *Companionship.* The affection, love, and true companionship which grow out of a oneness of spirit as each partner models Christ's unconditional love (Amos 3:3).
2. *Enjoyment.* The physical relationship is a reflection of the loyalty and affection shared among marriage partners who have become "one flesh" (Hebrews 13:4).
3. *Fruitfulness.* The blessing of children in a marriage relationship allows that relationship to reproduce itself physically. It is an example of the "oneness" that results in a marriage (Genesis 1:28; 1 Peter 3:7).

4. *Protection.* The husband protects the wife by laying down his life for her (Ephesians 5:25). The wife is to protect the home (Titus 2:4–5), and the parents together protect their children to raise up a godly generation (Malachi 2:15; Psalm 112:1–2).

When secondary purposes for marriage are placed above the primary purpose, discontentment, fearfulness, and disillusionment often result. Jesus desires to guide both the husband and the wife into places of fruitfulness and fulfillment that only he can provide in their individual relationship with them.

I would like to give a word to singles right here. Your singleness is an incredible blessing to the kingdom when it's surrendered to Christ. Don't waste your singleness on being discontent; Jesus wants to help you discover riches in your singleness that you will never be able to go back and recapture in married life. There is joy, spiritual fulfillment, and intimate companionship with Jesus that will meet every need in your singleness.

It's in your singleness that you learn how to surrender your will to the word of God, you learn how to discipline your desires to godliness, you develop a sense of purpose birthed out of prayer and devotion, and it's in your singleness that you learn how to encourage yourself in the Lord when no one else is encouraging you.

There is a practical and spiritual resource you offer to the kingdom of God through your singleness. This is a time to be an armor barrier to the leadership of your church. Don't allow the enemy to convolute your life to the point of distractions that spoil and rob your ministry of the gift-ings that God has placed in your life. There is a preparation in your singleness that is time-sensitive to this season in your life no matter how long or short; use it for God.

When you read the thirteenth chapter of 1 Corinthians, you'll discover a fascinating description of love—the kind of love that is possible for every Spirit-filled believer to have. You will see that one thing love does is wait. It is patient. Therefore, you shouldn't worry that you might become an "old maid" or be a "bachelor brother" all your life. If you continually delight yourself in the Lord and seek always to please him, he will give you the desire of your heart. It is your heavenly Father's good pleasure to give you his bless-ings. *You are living in a place of significance in your singleness; don't minimize the importance of who you are right now, or miss out on a vibrant love relationship with Jesus while you are single.* This reminds me of the poem by Gorge D. Watson.

> I am crucified with Christ: neverthe-less I live; yet not I, but Christ liveth in me: and the life which I now live in the flesh I live by the faith of the Son of God, who loved me, and gave himself for me. (Galatians 2:20)

If God has called you to be really like Christ in all your spirit, he will draw you into a life of crucifixion and humil-ity and put on you such demands of obedience, that he will not allow you to follow other Christians, and in many ways, he will seem to let other good people do things which he will not let you do.

Others can brag about themselves, and their work, on their success, on their writings, but the Holy Spirit will not allow you to do any such thing, and if you begin it, he will lead you into some deep mortification that will make you despise yourself and all your good works.

The Lord will let others be honored and put forward, and keep you hid away in obscurity because he wants to produce some choice fragrant fruit for his glory, which can be produced only in the shade.

Others will be allowed to succeed in making money, but it is likely God will keep you poor because he wants you to have something far better than gold, and that is a helpless dependence on him; that he may have the privilege of supplying your needs day by day—out of an unseen treasury.

God will let others be great, but he will keep you small. He will let others do a great work for him and get credit for it, but he will make you work and toil on without knowing how much you are doing; and then to make your work still more precious, he will let others get the credit for the work you have done, and this will make your reward ten times greater when he comes.

The Holy Spirit will put strict watch over you, with a jealous love, and will rebuke you for little words and feelings, or for wasting your time, which other Christians never seem distressed over.

So make up your mind that God is an infinite sovereign, and has a right to do what he pleases with his own, and he will not explain to you a thousand things which may puzzle your reason in his dealing with you. He will wrap you up in a jealous love, and let other people say and do many things that you cannot do or say.

Settle it forever, that you are to deal directly with the Holy Spirit, and that he is to have the privilege of tying your tongue, or chaining your hand, or closing your eyes in ways that others are not dealt with.

Now when you are so possessed with the living God that you are, in your secret heart, pleased and delighted over this particular personal, private, jealous guardianship and management of the Holy Spirit over your life, you will have found the vestibule of heaven. (G. D. Watson)

For to me to live *is* Christ, and to die *is* gain. (Philippians 1:21)

So then every one of us shall give account of himself to God. (Romans 14:12)

Reflection questions:

1. Do I put value on my spouse input or concerns? If not, why don't I?
2. Do I allow the word of God to govern my attitude and the way I speak to my spouse?
3. Am I putting more value on the secondary purposes of my marriage relationship than the primary purpose of glorying God through our marriage?

CHAPTER 3

Wielding Weapons versus Using Tools

With tear-filled eyes and her voice breaking, Nancy says, "I've tried everything to get him just listen to me without him talking over me, but he just gets aggressive and loud. I don't know what to do any more, I feel it's useless."

Her husband, Tim, sits next to her on the couch, obviously angered by her words, but silent. Finally he speaks after what seems to be a break in her emotional rant. He starts off, "Doesn't the Bible say something about wives submitting and respecting their husbands? How can I lead in our marriage if she never listens to anything I tell her? She's the one with the problem because she never listens."

I listen as they explain how hard it had become to even be in the same room, much less the same house, with each other.

Once they've settled down a bit and looked at me, I began to explain to them how hard it is to have success in their conversation when they bring weapons to the bridge instead of tools. If Nancy feels that the only way she can be heard is by using emotional manipulation, and Tim feels that the only way he can get respect is by using intimidation, they both have brought weapons instead of tools to the bridge.

Nancy's first approach toward Tim should be that of a partner: "Tim, I'm sorry if I come across inconsiderate to you in any way. My desire is to share my heart on this issue and how it affects me. I need your help and understanding to help me manage my emotions and respond correctly to you. Would you please be patient and partner with me as I work this out?" That approach will build confidence in Tim and make him a partner in solving a problem, which men love. Men are innately fixers, conquerors of the insurmountable heaps that challenge their will and strength.

Tim's approach toward Nancy should be in the spirit of grace: "Nancy, I can tell you're upset, and that's not what I want. I want you to share whatever is in your heart and know that I'm here for you. If I've done anything that has communicated differently, I'm very sorry." That approach will open Nancy up to honest discussion and make her feel like Tim cares about the concerns of her heart. Women will close up if they think they're going to be intimidated in a conversation. Elevated tones and aggressive gesturing are the worst approaches to getting honesty out of or from them.

Unfortunately, couples can easily do more destroying of bridges in their marriages than building or restoring. This is often because of lack of understanding, pride, and previous failed expectations that cause us to defend and protect our position at all costs. So we bring all of the wrong tools to the bridge; better yet, we don't bring tools but weapons.

Our words become as dangerous as a grenade, our attitude as toxic as a poison that permeates the air around us.

I've counseled many couples who have had no clue that that each time they come to the bridge of their marriage, they are weaponized against each other, and communication becomes a place of anxiety. They have conditioned each other to come weaponized to every conversation. Trust and respect are nowhere to be found because both are tired, angry, and defensive.

Amos 3:3 asks an important question: "Can two walk together, except they be agreed?" But scenarios like Tim and Nancy's are common when both spouses are more focused on why they're upset with each other than solutions to make things better. They meet on the bridge not to agree but simply to claim victory, professing their entitled position of rightness over the other. Neither brings anything to the bridge that will calm the storm that is about to turn into a hurricane. It's very important to understand what tools are needed in the different stages of bridge building, bridge restoring, and sustaining confidence of the bridge's integrity.

Dr. John Gottman, a professor at the University of Washington, wrote about the five weapons couples bring to the bridge, thus assuring their own destruction. These weapons represent dangerous and wrong ways to communicate. Next to the explanation of each of Gottman's weapons, I offer a tool as an alternative.

	WEAPON: Criticism	TOOL: Affirmation/ Compliments
What it looks like	Makes the other feel like they cannot do anything right, and it demoralizes their efforts.	Sweetheart, the thing I love about you is your kindness and patience. I don't think I could have the courage to do this without you.
What its effects are	The other person feels inadequate, and it covers the person in shame. Criticism breeds contempt.	Thank you for being understanding and caring.

	WEAPON: Contempt	TOOL: Esteem/ Respect
What it looks like	Intention to insult and abuse the other person with words. Words are wielded like a bat: calling names, making fun of, putting down.	I want you to know how much I value your opinion. If I ever say anything that makes you feel less than loved by me, I apologize.

What its effects are	Inner pain and scarring. Contempt breeds defensiveness.	(fill in the blank)

	WEAPON: Defensiveness	TOOL: Sympathy/ Apologies
What it looks like	Not wanting to confess wrongdoing. Doesn't want to take ownership of own actions. (It is always someone else's fault.) Oftentimes, an attitude of "You make me do this."	A gentle touch is very important when discussing painful or challenging topics. Give your full attention, looking the other person in the face, showing empathy.
What its effects are	(Fill in the blank) Defensiveness breeds stonewalling.	Never turn your back to the other person when talking to them.

	WEAPON: Stonewalling	TOOL: Open Communication
What it looks like	Cold unresponsiveness, just like a stone wall. Nonparticipation when working on the issues.	Try not to come to a stressful conversation with a scowl or frown. Have questions written down that you want to discuss. (Fill in the blank.)
What its effects are	Abandonment	(Fill in the blank.)

	WEAPON: Selfishness	TOOL: Sacrificial Selflessness
What it looks like	Making your relationship all about "me" and "I." Never considering how behavior affects your spouse. Setting up a wall/boundary around "me" and "my needs."	Making your relationship all about "her" or "him." Always considering how your behavior affects your spouse. Setting up a wall/boundary around "us" and "our needs."
What its effects are	(Fill in the blank)	(Fill in the blank)

When two people on separate sides of a bridge meet in the middle, there should be a productive outcome that glorifies God. The bridge is a vivid picture and a focus point to remind us to disarm before discussing issues that could blow up and destroy communication.

We bring who we are, not just information or reason, to every conversation we have. Our outlook and expectations will drive our thought process as we conversate on any given topic. If we're already at a point of frustration or anxiety before we go into discussions, we need to slow down for true self-assessment of how we're coming across to the other person. We tend to be less aware of our own disposition or spirit when we are processing failed expectations from our spouse.

Though you may have a right to be upset or even angered by circumstances, remember the point of the conversation is to bring solutions, and give God something to work with to restore peace and harmony to the relationship.

One important thing that Tim and Nancy didn't know—and that we should always keep in mind—is that the spirit of the conversation often speaks louder than the topic of the conversation. The enemy is always looking for an open door in our conversations to contaminate good intentions and disrupt harmony in the marriage by triggering us in our emotions to be unguarded with our words. Our words are spiritual in effect and need to be guarded in all conversations.

Paul talks about this in Ephesians 4:29:

> Do not let any unwholesome talk come out of your mouths, but only what is helpful for building others up according to their needs, that it may benefit those who listen.

So before you enter into any stressful or challenging conversation—or any conversation, really—remember the image of the bridge, then ask yourself, "Am I bringing weapons or hope to this conversation?"

We looked earlier in this chapter at some tools that are helpful for bringing hope instead of despair when building bridges across two people. Let's look now at some hardware—some pieces that can be used to both build and repair bridges as necessary.

Humility. From the biblical point of view, humility is the stooping of oneself to serve another; not thinking more highly of one's opinion or status over another; being able to be taught or led in a different direction by another. If we bring this tool each time we come to the bridge in any capacity, it will disarm most arguments and make room for God's intervention and promote positive outcomes.

Anytime we find ourselves feeling the need to persuade the other person to our point of view only, humility is no longer present. Humility says, "How I can help alleviate your pain?" and "How can I work with you?"

When it's our way or the highway, we push our spouse into a combative or isolated posture by the very nature of disrespecting who they are, and what they bring to the relationship. Marriage requires us to be both teacher and student if we desire to be successful in the long haul. I'll speak more on that later in the book to explain my point. Humility is sometimes confused with practiced and polished tactical skills of winning an argument. Measured tone, calm yet smug demeanor, and sarcastic replies to questions asked are not signs of humility. These are very clear signs of someone doing their best to manipulate and control the conversation, while dismissing any valid concerns the other person has.

This kind of behavior will demoralize your spouse and kill any hope of coming together on any cause. Humility means communicating in love, being willing to forgive, and loving above all else.

Respectful attention. Often, we come to the bridge with preconceived or biased ideas of the outcome we expect to get. This can be because of history established already in the relationship, or history prior to the relationship. It's very hard to hear or see anything new when our minds are filtering words and expressions from a familiar place of disappointment. So our attention span for what's been said or communicated is distracted at best, and cold or disconnected at worse.

When we're unable to hear with a listening heart, or see with fresh eyes on the bridge of communication, our attention is already elsewhere, and it communicates a lack of respect to our partner. Here are some tips for active, respectful listening:

1. Touching. Every so often, touch the other person's hand while talking to communicate connection and sincerity. This sometimes can be strained depending on the severity of the discussion. (But don't force this on your spouse if they're emotionally triggered and need space to process their feelings.)

2. Respect what you see in front of you. I often asked couples to bring a mirror to their conversations to assess body language. Turning away while your spouse is talking, or walking away, is not respecting who's in front of you.

3. Put away electronic and technical devices when having conversations. Make the person in front of you more important than your phone or tablet.

4. Consider whether you have time to discuss an issue before bringing it up. It's not smart to bring up a topic or issues right before you're walking out the door for work, for instance. Some couples find it helpful to schedule conversations; the key is to communicate and find a time that works for both of you.

How we listen will determine how we react or respond to what's being said.

Measured language. Scripture says in Proverbs 15:1, "A soft answer turneth away wrath: but grievous words stir up anger."

Why is it so easy to be unguarded with our language when we're talking with our spouse? James 1:26 says, "If anyone among you thinks he is religious, and does not bridle his tongue but deceives his own heart, this one's religion *is* useless." It's called conditioned familiarity, the training of oneself in the discourse of strained communication, forming habitual behavior. For example: If you've been conditioned to argue because that was the only way you felt your voice was heard, you bring contention to every conversation without even thinking about it. If your spouse disagrees with you, and it's an automatic confrontation that leads to hurtful words and you defending your position, most likely there is a lack of discipline and understanding in the way you approach communication. In marriage, it's important for couples to understand that it is okay if your spouse does not agree on every issue. As long as it isn't an issue of morality or ethics, it's okay to have a difference of opinion. When you can give an account to your perspective, it should be respected.

We are naturally creatures of habit; the more we practice something, the more it becomes a part of our behavioral instinct.

The words we use with our spouse will create a culture of trust and support in our relationship, or they will create an atmosphere of frustration and insecurities. Our language is a reflection of our thoughts, which reveal the disposition of our hearts.

Negotiation/Compromise. The root meaning for the word "compromise" is *mutual promise.* If we keep this in mind when trying to establish a compromise, we will inevitably have consideration for our spouse in our approach for a compromise.

Consider Ephesians 2:11–22:

> Wherefore remember, that ye being in time past Gentiles in the flesh, who are called Uncircumcision by that which is called the Circumcision in the flesh made by hands; That at that time ye were without Christ, being aliens from the commonwealth of Israel, and strangers from the covenants of promise, having no hope,

and without God in the world: But now in Christ Jesus ye who sometimes were far off are made nigh by the blood of Christ. For he is our peace, who hath made both one, and hath broken down the middle wall of partition between us; Having abolished in his flesh the enmity, even the law of commandments contained in ordinances; for to make in himself of twain one new man, so making peace; And that he might reconcile both unto God in one body by the cross, having slain the enmity thereby: And came and preached peace to you which were afar off, and to them that were nigh. For through him we both have access by one Spirit unto the Father. Now therefore ye are no more strangers and foreigners, but fellow citizens with the saints, and of the household of God; And are built upon the foundation of the apostles and prophets, Jesus Christ himself being the chief corner stone; In whom all the building fitly framed together groweth unto an holy temple in the Lord: In whom ye also are builded together for an habitation of God through the Spirit.

So often, we are left with limited responses because we've not taken the time to understand why we're at the bridge again. Most of the time, we're at the bridge because one or both spouses feel misunderstood, and this misunderstanding has caused tension that can no longer be ignored.

Proverbs 18:19 says, "A brother offended is harder to win than a strong city." Once an offense is established in the heart, it is hard to navigate your behavior around the offense. The common thing to do is to set up defenses and work on your argument. If your goal is to win at all costs no matter the damage, be assured there will be damage. Compromise requires surrendering our perception of what we think should happen, to make room for the other person's expectations.

If you can keep a heart of compassion toward your spouse, the chances of coming to a compromise that is workable in the relationship is very possible.

If our offense is so great that compassion is gone, arguing will take the place of conciliation and will further justify our defenses, creating an atmosphere of individualism that will take us further and further apart.

Next time your spouse offends you, ask yourself this: Are you so offended that you would rather have someone else by your deathbed? That might sound harsh or even morbid, but it's the reality of how we allow things to become so toxic that we lose sight of the larger picture.

The enemy's goal is to sow seeds of division in your marriage at any cost, in every area of your relationship. It's our job to expose him and keep him out our hearts so we don't become a weapon against our marriage.

Let's ponder on these words from Scripture as we close out this chapter:

THE BRIDGE BETWEEN US

None of us know our faults. Forgive me when I sin without knowing it. Don't let me do wrong on purpose, Lord, or let sin have control over my life. Then I will be innocent, and not guilty of some terrible fault. Let my words and my thoughts be pleasing to you, Lord, because you are my mighty rock and my protector. (Psalm 19:12–14)

Do not let any unwholesome talk come out of your mouths, but only what is helpful for building others up according to their needs, that it may benefit those who listen. And do not grieve the Holy Spirit of God, with whom you were sealed for the day of redemption. Get rid of all bitterness, rage and anger, brawling and slander, along with every form of malice. Be kind and compassionate to one another, forgiving each other, just as in Christ God forgave you. (Ephesians 4:29–32)

Reflection questions:

1. Am I ignoring the effects my words and actions have on my spouse?
2. Do I consider where I'm at in my headspace before hard conversations?
3. What tool or tools do I bring to the bridge?

CHAPTER 4

Seeing Jesus as the Bridge

I've read many good books on marriage, explaining how to get on the road to having a good marriage, by many great authors. I find myself agreeing with them most of the time when they start and conclude on biblical principles from God's word. When it comes to the topic of "becoming one," though, I think we can get a little heavy with a theological approach, often ignoring the practical application of Christlikeness.

Having been a preacher of God's word for twenty-five years, and using God's word to instruct, equip, and strengthen couples in their marriages, I've come to the conclusion that the work of becoming one in marriage must be a deliberate pursuit by both partners. This does not happen because one or both parties have good intentions on having a good marriage. It does not happen because one or both attend church and profess a relationship with Jesus. Until both begin to walk in a surrendered state of selflessness to please the Lord, becoming "one" will only be good intentions.

Let's take a look at what Jesus himself said about marriage:

> And he answered and said unto them, Have ye not read, that he which made them at the beginning made them male and female, And said, For this cause shall a man leave father and mother, and shall cleave to his wife: and they twain shall be one flesh? Wherefore they are no more twain, but one flesh. What therefore God hath joined together, let not man put asunder. (Matthew 19:4–6)

Marriage is between a male and a female! One male is joined to one female. There is a leaving behind of family. There is a cleaving together. They become one flesh. According to God, they are no longer two but one. And God said let no man divide this union.

This is God's definition of marriage! Are you thankful that we have a record of what God says is right?

It is important to study the reason that God created marriage. Man's reason for marriage is often not God's reason for marriage.

Over the years, man's reasons for marriage have become warped: In an article "The Case of William F. Ogburn," he describes very clearly our need today in a godly marriage. Written by Robert C. Bannister, sociologists will tell you that the institution of marriage grew as man evolved because rogue males needed to be domesticated.

DR. RICK D. MERRITT

In order for a female to capture the attention of a wild male and keep him interested long enough to raise children, some sort of religious ceremony had to be invented. Marriage became a way to civilize men.

But that is not what the Bible says at all. Let's go all the way back to the beginning, to Genesis 2:18–24:

> And the Lord God said, "It is not good that the man should be alone; I will make him an help meet for him." And out of the ground the Lord God formed every beast of the field, and every fowl of the air; and brought them unto Adam to see what he would call them: and whatsoever Adam called every living creature, that was the name thereof. And Adam gave names to all cattle, and to the fowl of the air, and to every beast of the field; but for Adam there was not found an help meet for him. And the Lord God caused a deep sleep to fall upon Adam and he slept: and he took one of his ribs, and closed up the flesh instead thereof; And the rib, which the Lord God had taken from man, made he a woman, and brought her unto the man. And Adam said, "This is now bone of my bones, and flesh of my flesh: she shall be called Woman, because she was taken out of Man. Therefore shall a man leave his father and his mother, and shall cleave unto his wife: and they shall be one flesh."

God said it was not good for man to be alone; he needed help. God said, "I will make a helpmeet for him." Remember that word. The reason that we get married is because God created a perfect partner for man. The man and the woman were designed to help one another.

The man was not created for the man, or the woman for the woman. But the woman was created for the man, and the man for the woman.

The Hebrew word for helpmeet is *neged* which means "a counterpart" or "mate." The world lends itself to opposites; a counterpart is something that works in conjunction with another part; it does not work alone. The man and the woman were originally designed by God as counterparts; one does not work to his or her ultimate potential without the other. In fact, God's plan in marriage is two counterparts working together as one.

This is part of God's design; in a nutshell, this is the reason for marriage. Marriage was, and is, part of the creative work of God. It is an amazing thing to be able to enter into this creative work of God.

Marriage is unique in that it displays the character of God to mankind. The love that is displayed in marriage reflects the love that God has for his church.

There are three phrases in Genesis 2:24 that we need to examine, because they are the foundation of marriage.

Therefore shall a man leave his father
and his mother, and shall cleave unto his
wife: and they shall be one flesh.

God's purposes for marriage are related to the original oneness and harmony of the wonderful reflection of God's image in all of creation. Leaving, cleaving, and becoming one is the foundation for every God-ordained marriage in the world.

Let's look at these three things one at a time: Leave father and mother. Cleave to one another. Become one flesh.

Leave his father and his mother

The Scripture actually says that a man should leave his father and his mother. In Bible times, and in most cultures, it was typical for the woman to leave her home of origin and be united with her husband. Even living with the man's family was quite normal. It is significant here that God calls on the man to leave father and mother. By focusing on the man, God makes the case that leaving takes place for both the man and the woman. So, men, you do not have to live with your in-laws, and neither do you, ladies. The leaving is an important part of marriage. This is the very first part of marriage, leaving behind those things you have counted on. You are entering into a brand-new phase of life, and it begins when you leave your father and mother. In modern vernacular, we could call this growing up, becoming an adult!

Hopefully, your parents have prepared you for this day all your life while at home. It is time to leave. It is time to provide for yourself and your wife. It is time to be an adult. It doesn't always happen overnight, but it must happen for marriage to be successful.

We know that this is not a separation from our parents. We are still family. They will be there for us when we need them. If they are living, they may even help us from time to time. Good parents will do that. Yet it is part of God's plan for you to make it on your own.

Each of us is different, and sometimes leaving is a process that takes time. Sometimes it is necessary and beneficial to live with family for a time, for specific reasons. Still, God said the leaving must take place; it is part of marriage.

Take what you have learned and put it to use. If you had or have terrible parents, you will only benefit from leaving. If you had or have abusive parents, leave behind the hurt and pain. If you had or have great parents, thank the Lord and try to emulate them in your own life.

Cleave unto his wife

The second part of our text says, "Cleave unto your wife." There is the leaving, and then there is the cleaving. Cleaving means the joining together. This is not referring to a physical act of intimacy. This is referring to the mental, emotional, and spiritual makeup of a marriage.

There must be a joining together. This is a lifelong process. This goes way beyond the marriage vows. Actions speak louder than words here. Both the man and the woman must make a choice to unite this relationship.

If anything enters that may weaken the union of marriage, both the man and the woman must work toward strengthening it again. Laughing together. Helping each other. Sharing openly.

DR. RICK D. MERRITT

They shall be one flesh

The third point our text makes is, "And they shall be one flesh." God has ordained that this takes place only in the marriage union between husband and wife.

There is much more to becoming one flesh than a physical act of consummating the marriage through the sexual act on the wedding night. What happens at the physical level should happen at every level of the relationship: body, soul, and spirit. Your souls become one, soul mates. Your thinking is joined; be of the same mind considering one another (Philippians 2:2). Your emotions are joined, esteeming the other over yourself (Philippians 2:3).

Part of God's creative work is making two into *one* in marriage. Some doctors and therapists will tell you that what affects your body doesn't necessarily affect your spirit, or what affects your mind does not affect your soul.

Yet the Bible says out of the abundance of the heart, the mouth speaks. Our emotions, our mental thought process does affect us physically and spiritually. There is no separation. Why do you think the scriptures are so concerned about sexual immorality? Those kinds of choices have enormous repercussions for your spiritual and mental state in the marriage relationship.

That is why it is God's will for you to give all of yourself to your spouse in marriage. This process of becoming one flesh takes a lifetime to achieve. You can't really be united to somebody in a few years. This process takes place over your lifetimes!

Every marriage is made up of unique individuals, so every marriage is unique in its own right. Each marriage will have its own challenges; still, every couple must find a way to become one flesh in their marriage relationship.

Some marriages are filled with so much activity and driven agendas that their marriage looks like a high-stakes business deal with little room for mistakes. Those marriages need to slow down and enjoy the process of becoming one.

Some marriages look like love stories: the perfect couple, like a perfect piece of poetry, no fights, no problems, no bad days. Everybody stands back in wonder and awe, thinking, *How do they do that?*

I'm sure we've all seen couples like that and wonder what it is like to live in their shoes. Let me tell you, they are not really perfect, but there is something special about those marriages. They are simply enjoying the process of becoming one flesh. There's no competition in their relationship, only partnership.

Some marriages resemble bad weather, tornadoes, hurricanes, icy storms with blizzard winds. Others appear bliss with perfect west coast sunshine conditions. Each marriage is still challenged in its on way to become one flesh.

A word on wisdom

Following God's plan for marriage isn't always easy; in fact, it can be downright the hardest thing you might ever do in your lifetime. Even though God doesn't have an additional manual for personality types, he does have every answer you need in his word.

We should also keep in mind that unflattering behavior needs to be considered in the contexts of our spouse's personability. After all, there was something in their personality that made you want to fall in love with them. Proverbs 3:13–18 commends the ways of wisdom to us.

> Blessed is the one who finds wisdom,
> and the one who gets understanding,
> for the gain from her is better than gain
> from silver
> and her profit better than gold.
> She is more precious than jewels,
> and nothing you desire can compare with
> her.
> Long life is in her right hand;
> in her left hand are riches and honor.
> Her ways are ways of pleasantness,
> and all her paths are peace.
> She is a tree of life to those who lay hold
> of her;
> those who hold her fast are called blessed.

Wisdom: the soundness of an action or decision with regard to the application of experience, knowledge, and good judgment.

Wisdom is too often underrated in most relationships. If we apply this definition to our relationships, it would require the work of paying attention, listening, sacrificing, and learning our spouses. The Bible admonishes us to dwell in our marriages with understanding (1 Peter 3:7). This is the application of wisdom through experience. That means we must be active learners in our relationships in order to gain understanding that will benefit both ourselves and our partners.

I advise couples in premarital counseling to understand that in marriage, there will be times when you're the teacher, and there will be times when you will be the student.

The role of teacher or student will be determined by any given opportunity to listen to your spouse, or help your spouse understand your heart on an issue. Both roles require patience and grace, considering you are at each moment an instrument for God or the enemy.

Friend, be encouraged by this passage that shows how important it is to live together in unity and wisdom.

> Two are better than one, because they have a good return for their labor: If either of them falls down, one can help the other up. But pity anyone who falls and has no one to help them up. Also, if two lie down together, they will keep warm. But how can one keep warm alone? Though one may be overpowered, two can defend themselves. A cord of three strands is not quickly broken. (Ecclesiastes 4:9–12 NIV)

Reflection questions:

1. Do I approach the bridge in my marriage from God's word or my emotions?
2. Do I see my spouse through the lens of God's word or my experiences?
3. Do I invite Jesus to the bridge with me?

CHAPTER 5

Dancing across Bridges

Rhythm /rith-uhm/:

1. Movement or procedure with uniform or patterned recurrence of a beat, accent, or the like
2. Measured movement, as in dancing

I'm often amused at people who don't have rhythm. I'm talking about the simple clapping your hands on the downbeat of a song. It's amazing to see people find an inaudible rhythm that no one else hears except them, and clap to that beat. As funny as that can be to someone like me who plays percussion and understands rhythms, it's not funny when you see couples off rhythm spiritually, emotionally, and psychologically in their marriage.

Married couples pursing oneness will face many challenges simply because they are two different people with different backgrounds, and possibly different visions of what they think marriage should look like. One can have a rhythm of heavy metal, and the other can have a rhythm of

DR. RICK D. MERRITT

a ballad. Somehow, they have to bring those two rhythms together and make it make sense for them. They have to find a way to dance back and forth in unity across the bridge of their marriage.

So how do you get in rhythm with your spouse in the pursuit of oneness? Everything I've shared in the previous chapters should give some guidance and help, but because every relationship goes through seasons, you must pay attention to the season your marriage is in right now. Just like a dance, you have to listen to the beat and watch your feet in order to make transitions and stay in rhythm with your partner.

It's the unexpected transitions in marriages that get couples offbeat and out of rhythm with each other, and their preplanned goals. Couples who do not go into marriage with a committed plan that keeps them accountable to each other and to the word of God will drift into emotional chaos and tango with frustrations. Whether you're a person of faith or just trying to keep from singing the blues in your marriage—no matter who you are, or who you're married to—life will inevitably leave battle scars. I want to list a few things that will take you out of rhythm in your marriage.

Rhythm buster one: pride

We talked a couple of chapters ago about how humility is such a great piece of hardware for building our bridges. We're going to talk now about pride, and how it can make us stumble as we're dancing with our spouses across our bridges.

If we view communication in marriage as a bridge, and we are dancing across that bridge together, pride is the thing that makes one person think the entire dance is about him or herself. The prideful person dances on his or her own, expecting the other person to go along with it.

Pride originated with one of the angels. They were beings created by God, depended entirely on him, and were completely one with God and his will. Then the most beautiful angel of God's creation (Satan) decided that he did not need God. Since then, Satan has challenged God's will and purposes continually. His pride has been evident in man's heart since the fall of man in sin.

The topic of pride is so big I've broken it down into three parts: power, knowledge, and virtue.

The PRIDE of power. This kind of pride seeks autonomy, the need to control at all costs. It functions from a posture that will not capitulate or surrender control when things are not going its way. Pride doesn't make room for compromise and is very comfortable standing in opposition of common decency. The intoxication of power has historically plagued and tarnished human relationships from family to fellowships and every establishment of all kinds. The desire to control from a self-entitled position of authority will ruin the best of relationships.

For instance, the husband who feels the need to control his wife from an entitled position will damage his wife's self-worth and diminish emotional intimacy. The very attribute that provides closeness and trust which births intimacy is the very thing he is destroying by his need to control her for his selfish needs. Of course, this goes the other way around too; wives are just as capable of pride of power.

That need to control is not always easily identified in the beginning; it can be masked by deeds that appear to be thoughtful and caring. It's not until a difference of opinion opposes an agenda or a disagreement of ideas challenges a final word, that the pride of power raises its head. When this spirit comes to the surface, it comes for one purpose only: to intimidate and subdue all who oppose. All resources at its disposal will be used to quench the opposition, even at the cost of inflicting emotional, financial, and psychological pain.

This happens in marriage, families, churches, and organizations. What is hidden underneath the need to control is a behavioral dysfunctionality that can often be traced back to undeveloped coping skills from childhood.

The psalmist saw his own propensity to pride and prayed,

> Good and upright is the Lord; therefore he instructs sinners in his ways. He guides the humble in what is right and teaches them his way. All the ways of the Lord are loving and faithful toward those who keep the demands of his covenant. For the sake of your name, Lord, forgive my iniquity, though it is great. (Psalm 25:8–11)

The PRIDE of knowledge. This kind of pride thinks it knows and doesn't need to be added unto. It functions from a place of superiority and compares status or position to justify itself.

It can disguise itself as an agent of help, but its true nature is to establish a dependency on those under its influence. This spirit of pride sets itself apart by declaring its independence; it is unteachable and often disconnected from any source of accountability. In marriage, this type of pride is manifested mostly when one spouse has been walking with the Lord longer than his or her mate, or one declares that his or her calling has elevated them to a higher place of revelation in their walk with the Lord. This is usually a self-proclaimed declaration not spoken aloud until an argument or disagreement; this spirit is also empowered when there is a failure on behalf of their spouse.

In the evangelical church world, the man in most marriages has been elevated as the spiritual powerhouse of revelation and knowledge simply because he is the man. This can make way for an elitist's mindset that misrepresents the man as more or better and appointed by God himself. The church world justifies and confirms this use of authority with scriptures which point to man as being the head of the woman because she is the weaker of the two.

This is a misinterpretation of scripture and God's intention. Look at these verses:

For there is no partiality with God. (Romans 2:11)

This is not to say the man is not the head of the household; he just isn't the only one who can hear from and receive knowledge from the Lord. In other words, God is not looking past or ignoring the woman to pour out his wisdom and understanding.

> If any of you lack wisdom, let him ask
> of God, that giveth to all men liberally,
> and upbraideth not; and it shall be given
> him. (James 1:5)

Knowledge, especially biblical knowledge, is meant to be shared for partnership to strengthen efforts.

The PRIDE *of virtue.* This kind of pride thinks it is so good that it does not need forgiveness, or imputed righteousness. This is the sin of presumption—to think your past good deeds exempt you from present fault.

> For by grace you have been saved
> through faith, and that not of yourselves;
> *it is* the gift of God, not of works, lest any-
> one should boast.[2] (Ephesians 2:8–9)

So wherever you see a resistance to God, you will find one of these "prides" manifested in the human heart. When God describes pride, he describes it in malignant terms; it pervades the whole system. Pride doesn't allow us to compart-

---

[2]   *The New King James Version.* Nashville: Thomas Nelson Inc., 1982.

mentalize it to a single area of our life only. It will find expression in every area of our life, whether we desire it or not.

Is all pride bad? Let me just say that the forty-seven times it is used in the Bible, each time, it carries a negative connotation. Self-assurance should be accompanied with humility, so Jesus can be larger than our ego. God desires us to be confident and full of hope because of Christ in us, the hope of glory.

I think it's funny that we can practice humility easier in noncovenant relationships, but struggle to walk in humility in the marriage relationship. I think it's because superficial friendships really don't require our true selves to remain present and engaged. So we find ourselves acting most of the time, playing a part just long enough to keep the other person viewing us in a light that we project, to keep them thinking how great of a person we are. It's not until someone is seeing us on a daily basis that our guard slips and our true selves begin to show up. This happens at work, at school, and even at church. Most importantly, this also shows up after the honeymoon phase is over in marriage. Sometimes that phase is not long at all; it can literally be the first week of the marriage.

How often do we show our weakness upfront in our relationships? Believe it or not, this is exactly what we should do if we want to build a genuine connection to someone. You wouldn't hide a terminal sickness from someone trying to get close to you, so why would you hide any other weakness? This requires humility and courage, but it produces strength and trust in the relationship right away.

This is the problem with people who need control: most times, the reason they want to control a situation and other people around them is because they possess a weakness that taunts them and makes them feel unwanted or unloved. If they control the person that they're in a relationship with, they believe it keeps their weakness in hiding as long as they can point out someone else's fault.

Most times, prideful people have a lifetime of behavior behind them, and by the time they're in a relationship that requires them to be honest and transparent, they're unable because the cost is too high. They may not even know where to take the first step in being honest about who they are.

We may share offenses from our childhood in the beginning of the relationship when it benefits us in gaining sympathy or excusing us from an expectation in the relationship. We hardly ever share the subtle evasive offenses that shape and fashion our outlook on ourselves and life. Because they go unshared, when the relationship goes into deeper waters, these hurtful events remain unshared for the fear of rejection. But the deeper issues of those offenses remain protected and unprocessed because we've never felt comfortable putting them out in the open and trusting another person with our fears and pain.

I can't tell you how many times I've had couples sit in front of me and each share their childhood experiences, for me to find out it is the first time their spouse has heard the whole background story of their life.

This brings me to my next point that I mentioned earlier when addressing the issue of pride in marriage. PETs.

Personal emotional triggers: We all bring a trunk from our *past life* in marriage, often in it are all of the hurdles that will hinder the "becoming one" process. This trunk is hardly ever explored during the dating period or the engagement period. It remains untouched or acknowledged in marriage till chronic pain begins to change the emotional makeup of the marriage.

Normally when one or both spouses are walking on eggshells, and every conversation is laced with sarcasm and insult. The other position that I see often in marriages at this point is indifference.

Disappointment has taken front and center stage. "What's the use in trying? It's not going to make a difference." Indifference is very dangerous in the marriage relationship because it cools the heart and numbs our feelings.

We lose the ability to have genuine concern for our spouse; we have become isolated from them in our affections. This is mainly because we are triggered emotionally and don't know how to communicate our pain without feeling ashamed or vulnerable, and for most of us, it's the very first time in our lives we're honest about our pain. The reality is pretty shocking when PETs don't remain tucked away. Our defenses go up promptly when triggered without thinking or consideration of our spouse when an offense has somehow been made afresh in us. Not until we bring these things out in the light of God's word and speak his word over the offense and over us will we be free from the power of the offense. There are some personal issues even in marriage we will have to fight independently of our spouse. It's in marriage that we should have the support of our spouse to encourage us in those fights, undergird us in prayer, and provide grace in the struggle.

If you can't trust your spouse with your weaknesses because trust has been violated, then trust is the first thing that must be restored. This doesn't happen without deliberate steps toward that rebuilding process. Trust is the catalyst for the becoming-one blessing.

Rhythm buster two: unrealistic expectations

When one spouse is (or both spouses are) dancing with unrealistic expectations, they set the other one up for failure. You wouldn't expect a first-year ballet student to be the prima ballerina, and you wouldn't expect a hip-hop artist to dance the tango with no lessons. Similarly, you shouldn't expect things of your spouse that he or she cannot give.

You must dismiss the notion that marriage will complete you; people who think this way do not realize that marriage will not make a broken person whole. If anything, marriage will reveal the brokenness already existing in you.

There are a number of things that lead to unrealistic expectations, but the most common one is unspoken expectations. You expect your spouse to respond a certain way or do a certain thing simply because of the familiarity of the relationship. But just because you desire it and expect it from your spouse doesn't mean it is realistic. It is not realistic unless you have had the conversation about that expectation—AND your spouse has agreed to it.

Another way unrealistic expectations manifest is by demanding more than the other can give. For instance, if your wife gave birth three days ago, she will not be able to satisfy your sexual needs. You may have thought she would bounce back, but she will probably not be ready for that for several more weeks. Now is the time to swallow your pride, put her needs above yours, and dance at her pace.

You want success in your marriage, so you need to do the work that makes that possible. Talk about it, confirm it, commit to it and then partner together to see the success in it.

But let's step back for a minute and think about expectations in general. Expectations are things that we think we are owed (whether good or bad, big or little, rightfully or wrongfully so). We already discussed in the section on pride that the biggest thing we are rightfully owed is death or hell. But where does that leave us with our daily expectations, and how do we keep from becoming completely blasé about our relationship?

There's a difference between expectation and excitement. Expectations lead only to feelings of entitlement, despair, and disappointment, because they show that you are putting your hope in something besides Jesus. But it is totally okay to be excited: excited for what God is doing in your life, in your spouse's life, and in your marriage; excited that God gives good gifts; excited that your hope isn't in something temporary; excited that what God has done is enough.

What has God done that is "enough"? He sent his Son Jesus. Because of that, you can have certain expectations that will never make you feel entitled, never cause you to despair, and never disappoint you. You can expect

- to be seen as God sees Jesus (Hebrews 8:12),

- the Holy Spirit to be with you always (Joshua 1:9), and
- to be in heaven with God someday (John 14:2–3).

Basically, it's safe to expect whatever God promises through Jesus. Everything else—from who does the dishes, to who puts the kids to bed, to how often you want or need to be intimate with each other—all of that is something that is temporary, can change, and simply just needs to be talked through. And then, believe me, the dance that results from your marriage will flow freely and beautifully.

Rhythm buster three: unforgivable and unresolved offenses

If pride makes you dance by yourself, and unrealistic expectations make you demand something your partner cannot give, this rhythm buster makes you out of step with your partner. You may be dancing the same dance, in the same general vicinity, but unforgiveness and unresolved offenses make you constantly step on each other's toes and kick each other's shins, because you are just not in sync.

Forgive quickly, remember slowly. Unforgiveness will disturb any rhythm of peace and confidence in the marriage relationship. Unforgiveness is the only self-imposed challenge in the marriage that effectively pushes the other spouse out of the spiritual fight of the "oneness" concept.

Paul says in Ephesians 4:32, "Be kind to one another, tenderhearted, forgiving one another, as God in Christ forgave you." Forgiving one another keeps our marriage open to heaven's intervention so we can experience supernatural dynamics in every aspect of the marriage relationship. It keeps our heart and arms open to embrace our spouse, shutting the door on the enemy.

Unresolved offenses are different from unforgiven offenses. Unresolved offenses are those things that have been put on the shelf because one or both spouses do not want to work through the discomfort of apologizing for wrongdoing, and commit to change. Usually, one or the other spouse does not believe the offender is being sincere in their apology. This makes it really hard to move past the offense as a couple. The healthy process:

1. The offending spouse acknowledges the offense.
2. The offending spouse repents.
3. The offended spouse offers forgiveness to the offender.
4. Both spouses embrace hope to move past it.

Without this process, the offense will remain unresolved, creating distrust in the relationship. (One of the ways couples try to diminish unresolved offenses is with sex, but this only makes it worse for one or the other spouse because of the emotional scar[s] that exist[s] because of the offense. Sex does not fix emotional insecurities in your spouse, no matter how physically great it is.)

If your spouse is carrying around an unresolved offense in his or her heart, you may have to pay attention to the telltale signs. If they're easily triggered about the same thing, whatever that might be, is an area of disappointment and probably offense. The question you may want to ask yourself is, "Why does this bring contention every time?"

There may be times that you and your spouse cannot figure out where unforgiveness and unresolved offenses lie, or you may simply not know how to forgive or resolve the offense. In these instances, there is no shame in seeking out wise counsel—with the approval of your spouse, of course. This can be informal (talking with a close friend you trust), semiformal (meeting with a pastor or elder), or formal (sitting down with a professional therapist). Your pastor or elder may also be a licensed counselor; if not, he or she will probably have resources to point you to.

The Gospel of Luke tells us that one time, Jesus was eating dinner at the house of Simon, a Pharisee, when a sinful woman came up and began to wash Jesus's feet with her tears, and anoint him with oil. After a bit of conversation with his host, Jesus told Simon, "Her sins, which are many, are forgiven; for she loved much: but to whom little is forgiven, the same loveth little" (Luke 7:47).

Now whether you identify with the sinful woman or the self-righteous Pharisee, you have been forgiven much, by the very God of the universe, the Creator and sustainer of your life. God sent his only Son to the world so that you are free to *repent* and *forgive*. He forgives us, he enables our repentance, and he made a way for us to be reconciled to God, whom we broke fellowship with in the garden of Eden.

When you think of what Christ has done for you, it makes you free to do the following:

1. Repent to your spouse. Even if your part in the offense is only 1 percent, you can repent of that

1 percent, know that it is already paid for on the cross.

2. Forgive your spouse. Even if his or her part in the offense is 100 percent, you can forgive it all, knowing that it is already paid for on the cross.

Rhythm buster four: jealousy

In the marriage dance, the jealous dancer will always be looking around, afraid that someone else is going to step in. This causes the jealous dancer to lose focus on his or her spouse. They may be dancing together, but when the focus is taken off the dance and off the partner and placed elsewhere, the steps become out of sync, and your spouse is no longer the person you're trying to please.

When one or both spouses allow unabashed jealously into the marriage relationship, it creates the spirit of accusation, giving a foothold to the enemy to destroy their oneness. As a counselor, I find myself spending a lot of my time exposing what is being overlooked when the marriage relationship has fallen into disrepair.

Many times, there are legitimate reasons for a spouse to be concerned, based on behavioral history. A wife might say, "My husband is too flirtatious with other women," or "He's too touchy-feely and overly friendly with women." A husband might say, "My wife dresses too risqué when she leaves the house; she shows too much cleavage, and wears her clothes too short and too tight," or "It seems like she is trying to get other men to notice her." Usually paired with these serious accusations is the height of emotion. This

DR. RICK D. MERRITT

makes it difficult to substantiate the claims with truth so that healing can take place to help with any insecurity.

The first thing that needs to happen in instances of these claims is a pursuit of truth. Sometimes, the claims that cause jealousy are true, and sometimes they are not. We will look at each scenario here.

When the claims are not true: Too many times, I've found myself trying to make sense of a heartfelt description of wrongdoing as seen by one spouse, but with no factual evidence of the supposed behavior. If truth cannot be established because there is no evidence of the accusation, then the door to the enemy must be closed in the heart of the accuser. In most of these instances, one spouse feels insecure in the relationship because the other spouse is disconnected or unaware of their emotional and practical needs. So the disgruntled spouse gets jealous and points to anything negative to express their frustrations and disappointments.

When the claims are true: If there is evidence of the accusation, and a genuine history of wrong behavior of the other spouse, repentance and reconciliation are called for (see rhythm buster three). If the offending spouse will not acknowledge it, or is unwilling to make adjustments in their behavior to remove insecurities from their spouse, the couple needs to seek counseling. Sometimes, only one spouse is agreeable to counseling; in that instance, the other spouse should still seek counseling, and also talk to the elders of the church.

Conclusion, and a word about tempo

There is nothing more demoralizing in the marriage relationship than feeling disregarded and disrespected after you've shared your heart, and having been made to feel at blame for the actions of the person who is making you feel insecure. How do I overcome in my heart and mind? Love covers all wrong when we understand we are loved, then we can give love again and again with hope in our heart.

Tempo is important when it comes to rhythm. If you and your spouse function differently in your personal tempo in how you approach marriage, you will have issues in becoming one. Tempo is the personal temperament you bring to the relationship that will make it easy to dance with you, or make it difficult to stay in rhythm with you. Temperament is that thing that can be dressed up when we're trying to impress, but it's also the thing that will not remain hidden no matter how hard we try. A bad temperament can disrupt rhythm in your relationship because your spouse is constantly in contest of your outlook and behavior; but a good temperament can provide a cushion of grace to work through issues while trying to find your rhythm as a couple in the marriage. The challenge for rhythm in the marriage relationship is overcoming personal vices to make yourself compatible for partnership in the marriage.

Reflection questions:

1. Do I understand and consider the rhythm of my spouse?
2. Am I walking in humility on the bridge with my spouse?
3. Do I allow my PETs to demand unrealistic expectations?

CHAPTER 6

Showcasing Bridges

The glory of a good marriage is the attraction of attention received by family friends and the testimony of grace in the imperfection of brokenness. If they only knew the untold story of pain that God has been faithful to keep under his hand.

There is a spiritual aspect and application to the success of marriage that we need to remember in order to keep a healthy outlook on our role in marriage. When we look at our marriage through the lens of our flesh only, we disqualify ourselves from the supernatural intervention of God's help, and dismiss the possibility of demonic influences.

God created Adam and Eve not as an afterthought of his creation but to subdue Satan's challenge. It demonstrated to all of creation that only complete dependence on God results in true fulfillment of life.

Adam and Eve, and every person who followed, has a tremendous stake in God's plan and purpose for man. In this context, God gives three mandates for marriage: reflect, reign, and reproduce. These are, and have been, under assault from the very beginning of man's existence on earth. These are the very things about marriage that are under assault in our age.

Satan has been, and is still, very busy trying his best to pervert this trifold expression of God's plan for humanity. Let's take a look at why these are so important for the marriage couple to understand.

Reflect God's image

Christian marriages are to reflect God's image:

It is a serious thing to live in a society of possible gods and goddesses, to remember that the dullest most uninteresting person you can talk to may one day be a creature which, if you saw it now, you would be strongly tempted to worship, or else a horror and a corruption such as you now meet, if at all, only in a nightmare. All day long we are, in some degree, helping each other to one or the other of these destinations. It is in the light of these overwhelming possibilities, it is with the awe and the circumspection proper to them, that we should conduct all of our dealings with one another, all friendships, all loves, all play, all politics. There are no ordinary people. You have never talked to a mere mortal. Nations, cultures, arts, civilizations—these are mortal, and their life is to ours as the life of a gnat. But it is immortals whom we joke with, work with, marry, snub, and exploit—immortal horrors or everlasting splendors. (C. S. Lewis, *The Weight of Glory*)

Then God said, 'Let us make man *in our image, in our likeness,* and let them rule over the fish of the sea and the birds of the air, over the livestock, over all the earth, and over all the creatures that move along the ground. So, God created man in his own image, *in the image of God he created him; male and female* he created them.' (Genesis 1:26–27; emphasis mine)

Notice the emphasis on "image" and "likeness." God creates "them" as a unit to reflect him.

It takes both a man and woman, in oneness, to truly reflect his image in marriage. When we criticize our spouse, or foster division and competition, we are actually reflecting the disunity of Satan's disposition, and dishonoring God. On the other hand, when we recognize our purpose is to reflect the image of God, we are able to be convicted by the Holy Spirit to meet God's standard, and we guard our hearts toward one another. Criticism comes from resentment in our hearts often; the unresolved hurts and disappointments that remain fresh with aggregating thoughts that keep them alive in us. This can only be healed by us surrendering this weight to Jesus. "Come to Me, all *you* who labor and are heavy laden, and I will give you rest. Take My yoke upon you and learn from Me, for I am gentle and lowly in heart, and you will find rest for your souls. For My yoke *is* easy and My burden is light"[3] (Matthew 11:28).

---

[3] *The New King James Version.* (1982). (Mt 11:28–30). Nashville: Thomas Nelson.

If we have a bad or unhealthy image of ourselves, it makes it harder to see ourselves from God's perspective. If the enemy can diminish and devalue your self-image, he has successfully diminished the image of God in your marriage.

The more we look at our spouse as an opponent instead of partner, we stifle the "becoming one" process. Even though the process is hard at times, we must remember this is not a suggestion. God says, "Project my image."

Reproduce children in God's likeness

God's second purpose for marriage is to reproduce:

> God blessed them and said to them, *"Be fruitful and increase in number;* fill the earth and subdue it." (Genesis 1:28)

God's plan for married couples is to reproduce; bring forth "image bearers," children in his likeness. We should be very careful as Christians not to mix worldly wisdom, philosophy, and new age thinking in hopes of reproducing God's image. There's an image that God has for man that promotes his God-given identity; when we distort that image, we misrepresent the image of God. The command to reproduce his image has become an alternative.

Malachi told people of Israel:

> Has not the one God made you? You belong to him in body and spirit. And

> what does the one God seek? Godly off-
> spring; so be on your guard, and do not
> be unfaithful to the wife of your youth.
> (Malachi 3:15)

Our role as parents is to nurture, mentor, and develop our children according to God's word, that we may send them out to perpetuate what they've seen as his image, from our marriage, in the home. Couples who are competitive, angry, and divided are not fully able to nurture children in God's image. Why? In order to teach children the principles of αγάπε (agape: unconditional) love, godly discipline, and good morals, there must first be a display of becoming one in their marriage. Words are not enough!

As parents, couples must put aside their innate selfishness and fears, and trust God to help them be living examples of godliness, and put away petty disagreements for the sake of their children. The Christian couple who does not have children, or can't have children, can fulfill this purpose by making disciples of Jesus Christ where you have influence.

I have had couples ask me if it was wrong to not want children. There is no definitive biblical answer to this when it comes to marriage; because God has given the mandate to have children, with the blessing that comes with the addition of children, I recommend couples to pray together, not apart, about the will of God.

We live in an age that has twisted the view of marriage and the home according to God's original plan. When we except alternatives dismissing God's word, we agree with

an alternative of God's image. There are several conflict-
ing factors when comparing the will of God about marriage according to his word, the philosophy of our times
conflicts with the truth believers have been given in God's
word has the only image of marriage.

Reign in spiritual warfare

Married couples have the mandate to subdue and have
dominion as well as reflect and reproduce.

> God blessed them and said to them,
> "Be fruitful and increase in number; fill
> the earth and subdue it." (Genesis 1:28)

The enemy has known from the beginning that if he
can divide a home, he can divide its power and authority
against him. Read Jesus's words in the Gospel of Mark:

> How can Satan cast out Satan? And
> if a kingdom be divided against itself, that
> kingdom cannot stand. And if a house be
> divided against itself, that house cannot
> stand. And if Satan rise up against himself,
> and be divided, he cannot stand, but hath
> an end. No man can enter into a strong
> man's house, and spoil his goods, except
> he will first bind the strong man; and then
> he will spoil his house. (Mark 3:23–27)

As individuals, we are stewards of all resources entrusted to us, from the physical to the spiritual. We all have spiritual battles going on in our hearts at any given time. But when we come together in oneness, the enemy of our souls can be defeated. Just as the Godhead represents perfect unity and is a force for God's will in his universe, the Christian couple is to pray and discern God's will in all situations.

God has uniquely placed husband and wife together in agreement with God's will and with each other. As Paul states in Ephesians:

> For our struggle is not against flesh and
> blood, but against the rulers, against the
> authorities, against the powers of this dark
> world and against the spiritual forces of evil
> in the heavenly realms. (Ephesians 6:12)

Practically, our struggle is not against our spouse but against Satan who wants us to believe that our spouse is the problem. So here's the revelation the enemy doesn't want husband and wife to walk in: when we don't have an altar of grace in our marriage, we will ultimately end up partnering with the enemy in accusing our spouse when we should be exposing the enemy.

What does an altar of grace look like? The altar of grace in marriage is the place of elevation, a place to invoke God's involvement in any failure or disappointment that strains the relationship. It's a place to bring healing.

Consider with me the brazen altar God instructed Moses to build in the tabernacle experience, which was the precursor for the cross of our Lord Jesus. Just as in Numbers 21, in which the brazen serpent was lifted up as the symbol of redemption and healing, the altar brings us back to Christ in us the hope of glory, and the hope of God's intervention in any situation.

In Pastor Jack Hayford's book *A Time of Altars*, he lays out an excellent description of, and purpose for, altars. If we take the titles of his chapters in his book, we have a good look at why an altar of grace is so important in our marriages:

- A place of encounter
- A place of forgiveness
- A place of worship
- A place of covenant
- A place of intercession

If we consider each of these when it comes to our marriage, it will bring us back to center focus and alignment with the will of God for us in marriage.

I tell couples all of the time, "Sin should not destroy your marriage, for all have sinned and fallen short of being the perfect spouse" (Romans 3:23). This is not to excuse or pacify sin but to declare it defeated in Christ if we repent and turn away from it.

The problem that I've seen too often with Christian couples is complete condemnation of the spouse who has fallen into sin. In this instance, the enemy has not just won a victory over the one spouse, but has also infiltrated the marriage. If the offended spouse doesn't see this as an intrusion of the enemy, but simply as a failure of the offending spouse, the house is now divided. The enemy has done his job well because when one falls alone, woe to that person, but two can withstand him (Ecclesiastes 4:9–12).

This is not to trivialize or condone any offense or abuse anyone has suffered at the hands of their spouse, and I will talk more on the topic of abuse later in the book. I want to help you pull out of the emotional hurt long enough to engage your spiritual mind and strengthen your convictions. If your marriage is under spiritual assault—and there will be seasons when this will be the case—understand this will be the opportunity for you as husband and wife to stand together, not attack one another, and defeat the enemy. If you reign together in your marriage on spiritual matters, you will experience together the blessings of all things because of your marriage relationship.

If you are a Christian couple considering marriage, or one that has been married for a while, or maybe your marriage is in trouble, Jesus wants to remind you that a threefold cord is not easily broken. Remember you both are heirs of the grace of life.

Reflection questions:

1. Where can I partner with my spouse more on spiritual matters?
2. Have I adopted alternative mindsets apart from God's word about my role in marriage?
3. Do I provide an "altar of grace" in our marriage?

CHAPTER 7

Repairing Run-Down Bridges

As I stated earlier, most of us come into marriage with junk in our trunk. This does not mean that God is not going to help you, or should not relegate you to despair while trying to navigate through what's worth keeping or tossing away.

Most couples do not even know where to start making changes once they've come to the place they agree that change is needed. This can be in their communication, value system, or expectations. I've found out that if you can give a formula or some type of way to measure goals, it motivates and stirs for success. So consider this simple formula for walking in change. I call it the triple-*A* antidote for victory: awareness, acknowledgement, activation.

Awareness

Awareness \ə-ˈwer-nəs\: the quality or state of being aware; knowledge and understanding that something is happening or exists.

The first thing that needs to happen in making change is *awareness* of a problem. The very institution of marriage, according to the historical biblical ideological definition, is under attack all over the world. What I mean by this is marriage according to God's word, between man and woman. As Christians, when we stand in contrast to different expressions or ideas of a worldly or philosophical view of marriage other than God's definition, we draw demonic attention to ourselves. The enemy will seek opportunity through the husband and wife to find a foothold in the marriage. Perhaps one of the many challenges in evangelical Christian marriages can be linked to the enemy pulling strings in either the husband or wife, or both, to pit them one against the other. I believe this starts with entertaining a contrary thought to truth as we know it in God's word. When we do not pause long enough to consider that the enemy is NOT our spouse, we fall into the enemy's snare and do his bidding with our words, attitudes, and actions.

I'm always amazed that one or the other spouse isn't even aware that the marriage is in danger. To be aware is to awaken to the reality in front of you. The problem must first be exposed; it must first be seen before change is contended for by both the husband and the wife.

Most issues in marriage have a history of progression to them; these issues can be traced back to events brought into the marriage from previous experiences, or events which have happened within the current marriage relationship. Victory comes when both husband and wife agree that a problem exists, and agree to partner in overcoming the problem.

Unless both agree, the problem will continue to have power to create division in the marriage. For instance, if the husband is too distracted because he pours himself into his work or some other activity, he may be unaware of the stresses and strains in his marriage. This can be a frustration to his wife who is suffering alone trying to keep everything together. Similarly, if the wife is so independent in the way that she processes her anxieties because of past experiences, she may not trust sharing her feelings. This can produce insecurities in her husband and demoralize him in his efforts to fix or heal the problem. Both need to be aware of emotional triggers that exist in their spouse to work effectively in partnership for change. Awareness is crucial for success of change.

Acknowledgment

Acknowledge \ik-'nä-lij, ak-\: to disclose knowledge of or agreement with; to recognize as genuine or valid.

The next thing that needs to happen if we're going to walk in change is to acknowledge our role in fixing the problem. Until we recognize that we have a part to play for the success in marriage, we will ignore any role we have in the problem of the marriage relationship, and put blame on our spouse alone.

I've counseled many couples where it was pretty obvious that one or the other had committed offenses in the marriage. Unfortunately, this only empowered the offended spouse to sit in a place of judgment, to condemn his or her spouse. Whenever there is a breach of trust, or an offense has happened in the marriage, the marriage has had a weakness exposed. Something about the marriage relationship was exploited in either husband or wife or both. If couples cannot come to the place where they can say, "We have a problem in our marriage," neither will seek God independently for his grace to help them in the problem.

The marriage is designed by God in such a way that though you are individuals in a biological sense as man and woman, you are one unit in the essence of being. You have one identity from heaven's perspective. I often find that we do not want to acknowledge that there is something I could have added to the sin or weakness of my spouse. This is not to share blame of a wrong done by one or the other; this is to understand that because we are "one," I had to play a role in permitting, ignoring, facilitating, or aggravating the problem.

Listen, whether you are the initiator of the problem and you need to repent and ask for forgiveness, or you're the one who will not allow God to use you to bring restoration to the problem, both always have a role to play. You will hinder the restoration process in the marriage for bridging or healing unless you acknowledge you have a role to play in restoring the marriage to walk in strength and change.

Activation

Activate \ˈak-tə-ˌvāt\: to cause to function.

The third component in this module is activate. Once we are aware that there is a problem, and we acknowledge there is a role we play to help eliminate the problem, the next thing we must do is take responsibility and commit to action.

This can have many different expressions depending on the role God wants us to play, but there must be a willingness to act differently than we have in order to get different results in our relationship. After counseling couples for over two decades now, I've heard just about every excuse there is, why he or she has already done everything possible to make things better in their marriage. Couples are quick to declare how they've done more than their share with patience and prayer.

It is not that I disbelieve them or dismiss their sincerity, but in the statements "I've tried, I'm tired," or "I've done everything," what you're saying is "I've done my part." In other words, "Now I'm waiting for them to catch up with my efforts before I do anything else."

Holding grudges builds resentment toward our spouse, and numbs our sensitivity to the voice of God. It's in the hearing of God's voice that we experience conviction and find the courage to trust and act at the revelation of God speaking to us. This is why it is so important that we maintain a vibrant relationship with God.

Emotional pain will make us build walls and protect ourselves from what we perceive as potential harm if it's not surrendered to God. When it is given to God, we have a promise from his word that he will heal the brokenhearted (Psalm 147:3). What is the purpose of this healing? The same purpose of grace—so we can be strengthened to perform the will of God in our lives and in our marriages.

God always pays attention to our pain, but he also requires from us in our pain. I'm truly convinced that if we were to partner with God in our marriage, in the good times and in the bad, there is nothing that we can't overcome in the power of his spirit when he is helping us.

Conclusion

We need to remember this simple module at all times, because this can be the new way that we walk in if we want to live in victory and be the example of the power of God in Christian marriages.

Reflection questions:

1. Where do I need *awareness*? Do I allow my spouse to reveal my blind spots?
2. What area or areas do I need to *acknowledge* a need for change?
3. Am I being intentional to *activate* positive change when God shows me?

CHAPTER 8

Bridging the Gap through Love

The possibility that you can be with someone for years and not know what makes them feel loved and appreciated is a scary reality. Why is love often misinterpreted by feelings? Could it be because we've been conditioned to associate what makes us happy as the qualification of love? We are surrounded with visual and auditory stimulants that promote worldly and sensual wisdom that supports that definition. If we were to take a look at the word "love" in the Hebrew language, it may not surprise you to know that God's idea of love starts with himself. God so loved the world (creation) that he gave (John 3:16). This is the first expression of love, "to give"! (God gave himself because he loves us.)

Many good Christian teachers have written on the topic of love and its role in marriage, but I want to open you up to a deeper understanding of God's purpose of how this plays out with the creation of Eve. God understands that love can never be truly expressed until you have someone in your life whom you can love like God loves you.

This is why God says in Genesis 2:18, "It is not good that the man should be alone."

God, in his wisdom, gave Adam what he needed to reciprocate on Eve, his wife, what he first experienced from God. Woman was created to be the bridge that links man in every way back to God in his expression of how he loves his wife. This is why husbands are admonished to love their wives as Christ loves the church and gave himself for her (Ephesians 5:25). The woman is to be the gift whom the man loves, showing his connection to the love of the Father. In the same way, Jesus laying down his life became the bridge to restore that love relationship with the Father in heaven.

It is simple: we have a living, breathing person (our spouse) compatible to us in every way to bring out worship to God for his love toward us. This is why Adam and Eve are both made in the image of God, to show forth good works back to God in the oneness of loving one another.

Let's take a look at how love should be defined from God's wisdom. Love is the only human experience that can heal emotional brokenness. When there's emotional brokenness in the marriage, calisthenics is not what's needed. Counseling may help, reading the right book may help, sharing your heart may help, but the only thing that's going to heal that hurt is love. Here are some verses that talk about how seriously God takes the topic of love:

And we have known and believed the
love that God hath to us. God is love; and
he that dwelleth in love dwelleth in God,
and God in him. (1 John 4:16)

Be completely humble and gentle; be
patient, bearing with one another in love.
(Ephesians 4:2 NIV)

Above all, love each other deeply,
because love covers over a multitude of
sins. (1 Peter 4:8 NIV)

And now these three remain: faith,
hope and love. (1 Corinthians 13:13 NIV)

The woman needs love in its fullest expression because
she is designed to be a conduit or a doorway that connects
man back to God through his love toward her. She also nurtures and carries the seed of that love into the world through
giving birth. Though this is not her only expression of love
as a woman. She is by nature a nurturer in the marriage.

The woman's need for love is not only psychological or
emotional in the physical sense, but it is spiritual by origin
because of her designed role as the helpmeet (*neged*) that
completes man in his full potential spiritually. The woman
has been designed by God to thrive at her fullest potential
in the marriage when she's loved. Listen to what the word
of God says:

In this same way, husbands ought to
love their wives as their own bodies. He
who loves his wife loves himself. After all,
no one ever hated their own body, but they

feed and care for their body, just as Christ
does the church. (Ephesians 5:28–29)

God creating Eve for Adam was twofold: to populate
the earth, and to produce oneness (just as Adam was one
before Eve). God was teaching Adam that he would have
the opportunity to become one with his wife, connecting
back to God that way.

The word of God clearly outlines the husband's need
and role in marriage. Colossians 3:19 NIV says, "Husbands,
love your wives, and do not be harsh with them." This is
not vague or unclear at all. She is human with emotional
needs, physical needs, and spiritual needs. To ignore any of
her needs is to uncover her and leave her open to attacks,
which will draw demonic attention to the marriage union.
Husbands need to love their wives in every way that they
themselves experience love from God the Father. In this
way, they are in partnership with God to fulfill his plan and
his will. Husbands trying to function outside of that partnership with God in their marriage will set several destruc-
tive things in motion.

The effects are not always felt immediately, but when
they are manifest, they are not easily overcome, often taking much work to restore. I know at this point, some men
reading this chapter are asking the question, "What about
wives who bring the forbidden fruit into the marriage and
refuse counsel or do not yield their will to the word of
God?" How do you love and lead a woman who is bent on
getting her way at the risk of inviting demonic activity into
the marriage relationship?

I will be the first to admit that it is not easy to remain steadfast in humility and function in grace when your efforts to love are constantly rebuffed. Notice I said efforts to *love*, I didn't say efforts to *control*. Actually, quite commonly, the wife has been conditioned to behave a certain way, because of her husband's actions toward her! Trust has been violated, and that causes her to look past the husband to gain her self-worth and protect herself from further harm. This is why God states in his word,

> Likewise, husbands, live with your wives in an understanding way, showing honor to the woman as the weaker vessel, since they are heirs with you of the grace of life, so that your prayers may not be hindered. (1 Peter 3:7)

Once again, God is making it clear that the husband is accountable to God in his actions toward his wife. LOVE HER! She was given to you as a gift from God. Look again at what the word says: He who finds a wife finds a good thing and obtains favor from the Lord (Proverbs 18:22). Remember, this is a covenant relationship rooted in love. I think what most husbands fail to consider is this: God is trusting you with his daughter to heal, restore, and lift her out of emotional and psychological vices that might be in the background of her life. Marriage is meant to elevate her in every aspect of who she is as a woman through the way you love her. This is why she needs love, to be her best self in every way.

What does love look like to her?

It's very tempting right here to compose a list from things I've read in other great books on marriage, but I'm going to step out on a limb and try to answer this provocative question: "What does love look like to her?" Let me say upfront that if I tried to give a description of what it looks like to love your wife, I would at best be presuming, and at worst, reckless in my intentions.

She is your wife, and that question should be answered by you alone. Thank God for Gary Chapman's book *The 5 Love Languages*; I think he addresses the core psychological issues that reveal who we are when words are awkward or lost in the emotional moment trying to explain our frustration. But it's the journey of exploration with your wife that unfolds the questions: What does love look like to her? Are you listening to her when she speaks, are you asking questions that make her want to share her fears and insecurities, do you compliment her in her efforts and her appearance, do you do your best to fulfill her wishes when you know them? Would your wife consider you to be her best friend, or even a close friend?

You'd be surprised how often wives say they do not trust their husbands with their insecurities. This testifies that trust and communication have broken down in the marriage, or that they were never nurtured in the relationship from its infancy. A woman does not respond well to emotional bullying by their husband; if this is your approach for the sake of controlling her, you will bring to the surface one of two responses determined by her past experiences:

Sure, there are some cases when the woman will allow such behavior out of pure laziness, but in my twenty-five years of experience of pastoring and counseling marriages, one of these two cases will emerge.

1. A strong sense of self-worth fostered by her parents from her childhood. That response will look something like this if she detects bullying: "I need you to try to explain yourself without using childish tactics of yelling and throwing a temper tantrum. Let me know when you're ready to have an adult conversation." She is composed and confident, unimpressed with your behavior but will seek solutions. If bullying is used often by her husband, a loss of respect and trust is inevitable.

2. A low sense of self-worth fostered by her parents from childhood. Her background may be filled with rejection, trauma, bad decisions, brokenness, and insecurities. Her response to emotional bullying looks something like, "Who do you think you are, talking to me that way! I don't have to take this from you; you're not a man!" She's combative, confrontational, cutting, and argumentative because she has been triggered and reminded of past hurts. The absolute worst thing her husband can do is make her feel she needs to defend herself against him. If her husband continues to use bullying tactics, she will resign to a defensive disposition, inwardly broken into a million pieces, while outwardly going through the motions trying

to minimize her disappointment. But trust will be gone and hard to recover.

I know I haven't scratched the surface in my simple scenarios to illustrate a complete picture in either case, but you get the point. When the wife has a healthy self-assessment and strong emotional coping skills, she will be able to teach her husband what she needs in conversation, sex, and partnership. The husband in return will simply become the student that pays attention to get passing grades. If the wife comes into the marriage already recovering from or struggling with rejection, insecurity, and unresolved emotional trauma, the husband is the first line of defense that protects her from further insecurities. You must discover what love looks like to her by being patient and deliberately creating meaningful memories that overshadow the bad ones from her past. Don't expect her to give you a handbook on what to do; she most likely can only tell you what she doesn't want to experience because of her past pain.

If we are honest, most of us will admit that this type of love is not easy. Part of the reason for this is that we find it easier to be selfish than to be selfless. It is far easier for us to think about ourselves and our needs rather than the needs of those around us. When we live life in this way, however, those around us do not feel as though we truly love them. This is especially true when it comes to our spouses. One of the primary characteristics of godly love is that it is focused more upon others than upon ourselves.

Notice 1 Corinthians 13:5 when it says love "is not self-seeking." Indeed, Jesus said, "Greater love hath no man than this, that a man lay down his life for his friends" (John 15:13 NIV). Of course, this is exactly the type of love that Jesus showed for us! And this is the type of love that we need to show to our spouses as well.

How do we love like this in our marriages? How do we take practical steps to make our wives feel loved? Here are some answers to those questions, that I've discovered in my own marriage, and in my decades of marriage counseling. Disclaimer: not every wife is the same, so if you need to adjust some of these to meet your wife's particular needs, please do so.

Be confident, not arrogant. Brother, this means that you have to take charge without letting your pride overshadow consideration of others around you. It shows that you consider her when you're in public and you conduct yourself as a gentleman; confident in yourself, but not disrespectful in any way. Your wife wants to feel that her husband is emotionally secure so she can lean on you when she's emotionally insecure.

Take time to get to know her. The husband that can take his wife by the hand and navigate through the stresses of life while keeping his wife smiling with his sense of humor is a smart husband. Life can be difficult enough without having added anxiety because of an ill temperament.

Only make promises you can keep. Your wife wants a husband who will say what he means, and do what he says. Make no false promises. For instance, don't say you'll call if you don't have any intentions to do it, even if you think that's what she wants to hear.

That empty promise will cost more damage than good. You wife wants to know that your words are true. If she can't rely on your word, she will not trust you.

Remember, little things are a big deal. There is such a thing as a woman's intuition, and your wife probably has a healthy dose of it. She is watching when you think she is not, she is listening when you think she is not, she is comparing when you think she is not. She can't help it; it is her nature to want to measure up in your eyes. So when you open her door, help out around the house, help with the kids, get her flowers, or buy a card just because, it goes a long way. Do not do it to get something in return (trust me, she will know the difference); rather, make her feel like you are pleased to make her happy and take care of her emotions.

Keep the fire stoked with little acts of kindness so when you argue, the positives will outweigh the negatives, making it easier to forgive mistakes.

Tease her like she's precious. Most wives like it when you tease and flirt with them, when you make it fun for her; but if you take it past her comfort zone and she tells you, stop and apologize. Women like it when they sense a sincere apology that comes from the heart (and it will usually pay off in the bedroom!)

Make yourself appealing to her. Most women put a lot of effort into their looks. They want to look good with you on their side, so put some effort in your appearance also. Do your personal style, but look like you want to impress her. And if she gives you hints about going shopping, listen, and make it a fun opportunity for a date out. If she likes cologne, let her pick one for you. If she says you wear too much, listen to her. Whatever you do, you're doing for her, and it doesn't matter what others think or say.

Romance her. Stay classy; take her out just to talk to her; make her a queen for a day. Ask her about what's new in her life; get to know what's on her mind. Give her a reason to challenge herself intellectually, physically, and spiritually. You don't need to spend lots of money on her when she knows she has your attention. If you make her feel like a queen, she'll want to look and act like one.

Unburden her by taking responsibility. When the relationship gets challenged and stressed, which is inevitable, both of you need to take responsibility for the contribution of pain in the relationship. Don't say things that point the finger or blame. If you take the lead by admitting your fault, and remember it takes two to fight, most women will do the same. Make it easy by creating an atmosphere that makes her feel safe.

Listen, don't fix. I've found that when something is bothering them most, wives will talk about their feelings, their friends, and their day before they get to the real topic on their mind.

Your wife will share with her girlfriends or sisters if you are not giving her your ear, but she would probably rather share with you. She doesn't always need or want a solution. Sometimes she will just want you to just listen. So don't roll your eyes or interrupt, and don't offer your advice if she doesn't ask for it. If you don't know if she wants your advice or not, sometimes it is helpful to ask, "Do you want me to try to help, or do you want me to listen and/or pray for you?"

She knows you're a fixer, but sometimes all she wants is a sounding board. If you can give this respect, you will reap it in return.

Conclusion

If you commit your efforts to biblical principles, God will empower and guide you. His word provides us with a definition of love in 1 Corinthians 13. As you read through these verses, note that godly love is not just a warm feeling for someone.

> Love is patient, love is kind. It does not envy, it does not boast, it is not proud. It is not rude, it is not self-seeking, it is not easily angered, it keeps no record of wrongs. Love does not delight in evil but rejoices with the truth. It always protects, always trusts, always hopes, and always perseveres. Love never fails. (1 Corinthians 13:4–8a NIV)

This puts a whole new perspective on the meaning of the words "I love you!" Consider for a moment what this type of love looks like. "Honey, I love you. What I mean is I am patient and kind with you. I do not envy you, I do not boast in front of you, I am not proud before you. I am not rude to you, I seek your good and not my own, I am not easily angered by you, and I keep no record of your wrongs." If only we could love like this all the time!

Reflection questions:

1. Have I taken the time to KNOW her?
2. Is patience a consideration when working through issues?
3. Do I speak blessings over her with my words?

CHAPTER 9

Bridging the Gap through Respect

Being a male is a matter of BIRTH. Being a man is a matter of MATURITY. Being a gentleman is a matter of CHOICE.

When we consider the actual physiological and psychological makeup of males, it is obvious God had the presence of authority in mind when he created Adam. According to God in Genesis,

> And God said, Let us make man in our image, after our likeness: and let them have dominion over the fish of the sea, and over the fowl of the air, and over the cattle, and over all the earth, and over every creeping thing that creepeth upon the earth. So God created man in his own image, in the image of God created he him; male and female created he them. (Genesis 1:26–27)

The passage here is not androcentric or masculine based on gender dominion; it's descriptive from the one-ness of God's image transferred upon the man and woman. They were created to function in harmony as one, yet individually in their role, and their relationship to God.

The challenge to man's authority didn't arrive until after the fall. Before the fall, the Lord's plan was for a mutually interdependent relationship with both man and woman, where they would have constant communion with each other in harmony of his divine structure as husband and wife. But sin messed that up badly, disrupting what God had called "good" by perverting the nature of man and woman. Before I get to the point of why husbands need respect, let me establish why it is a real challenge and needs to be understood. Let's go to the word of God and find the challenge:

> Unto the woman he said, I will greatly
> multiply thy sorrow and thy conception;
> in sorrow thou shalt bring forth children;
> and *thy desire shall be to thy husband,* and
> he shall rule over thee. (emphasis mine)

There are different views on the meaning, "thy desire shall be to thy husband." One view on this is the woman's sexual desire will be for her husband. But keep in mind, this is supposed to be a curse. It was God who said it is not good that man be alone. To think he is going to curse Eve by giving her an abnormal or unhealthy desire for her husband sexually? That is not what God was communicating as her challenge, or as the consequence of her sin.

So let's take a closer look at the word desire in a scripture. In Genesis 4:6–7, we get a perspective: Cain's offering has been rejected by God, but his brother Abel's offering is accepted, which puts Cain in an emotional tailspin. His whole countenance has changed to the point that God addresses him with a warning: you better be careful to do what is right, sin is lurking at your door, its *desire* is for you, but you should rule over it.

The word desire in this passage is the same as in Genesis 3:16; it illustrates the picture of sin to dominate, to pounce at an opportunity. Could it be that God is warning the woman here of what sin has done to her spirit? You shall desire to dominate your husband and oppose God's divine structure for the family. A woman's desire for her husband is simply nothing more than a defiant attitude and disposition that pushes the man out of his place of leadership. This cascading effect of decline has been highlighted in several books on marriage already (Is there one you recommend in particular?) The natural progression of degradation in the fall of man is seen in the fact the woman was led by a creature, and man was led by his wife. Creation was out of sync and reversed in structure. The word *for* in our text can be translated to *against*.

The woman's desire because of the fall shall *be against* her husband's God-given position of leadership and authority. This will be the beginning of a perpetual struggle for woman embedded in her sinful nature. Her submission to a sinful man will be a difficult thing to do, but it is required of her by God. When the wife doesn't acknowledge her sinful impulses to subvert her husband's authority, she will be more susceptible to deception and the lies of the enemy, putting her in opposition of the oneness concept.

> Likewise, wives, be subject to your own husbands, so that even if some do not obey the word, they may be won *without a word* by the conduct of their wives, when they see your respectful and pure conduct. (1 Peter 3:1–2; emphasis mine)

The first attribute where a wife shows respect to her husband is with her words. It's with her words that she speaks, and the spirit that motivates her words, which will determine whether God or the enemy will use to build oneness in the marriage, or to tear it apart. I know this must be considered by both husband and wife, but this is magnified when the man's ego is bruised or torn down by his wife with her words. Consider Proverbs 6:2: "Thou art snared with the words of thy mouth, thou art taken with the words of thy mouth."

The lesson here is clear. When a wife's words are not measured and considered, they are used to wound and inflict pain to the husband and damage his confidence. More importantly, it is with her words that the wife removes herself from the order of divine blessings when she uses them to tear down her husband. She is in conflict with the very thing she wants: God's blessings and divine favor.

Naturally, the man is willing to deal with any battle or conflict outside his home; God has equipped him emotionally to withstand any threat or conflict to his person on his job, on the freeways, at the gas station, or any other place outside the home, specifically so he can fulfill his role as husband in the oneness concept. However, if his wife is argumentative and faultfinding, constantly instigating fights and fostering conflict, his wife becomes an opponent. His home is supposed to be a place of refuge, a place where he can be restored physically and spiritually. But when his wife is quarrelsome, it exhausts and zaps his strength; he becomes impatient and reacts in extreme ways to her treatment toward him when her words become a weapon to wound and insult him deeply. A wise wife will be mindful of her ability to build up or tear down her husband with her words.

Another area in which a wife can show respect is by not magnifying her husband's weaknesses.

> Who can find a wife of noble character? She is far more precious than rubies. The heart of her husband trusts in her, and he will lack nothing. She will bring him good and not harm all the days of her life. (Proverbs 31:10–12)

The wife that understands the importance of preserving her husband's dignity by not making him feel small in his struggles will create with her kindness and sensitivity a place of refuge in him, which she can come to in her own troubles and struggles. A wife like this understands clearly the oneness concept and presents herself as a partner to her husband, covering his blind spots with her kindness to preserve his ego.

She does what she can to create an atmosphere of love, respect, and peace in the home. And if it is necessary for her to point something out, she does it with grace and consideration, preserving her husband's ego and appointed place as leader of the home and family, giving him the benefit of following God in his decisions, surrendering her fears to God so she can be a support and pray for her husband.

Respect is the thread (woven into the marriage by the wife) that holds and honors her husband in his divine appointed place. If this thread is removed by the wife's conduct toward her husband, there will be an unraveling of the husband's trust in his wife, and the marriage relationship will suffer many challenges in the area of oneness. In short, the husband doesn't need respect to keep his ego in a safe place; if the wife doesn't honor her husband as God has called her to, she forfeits the blessing that comes with the divine order in marriage ordained by God. The wife who sees her husband through a kingdom lens will not lose sight of her role in partnering with God in her marriage.

I feel the need to explain what I mean by seeing through a kingdom lens. A large part of marriage is navigating through the practicality of life as a couple. The good, bad, and ugly come to the surface pretty quick when you are under the same roof every day and night. We can get so caught up in our version of a good marriage that we don't make room for God to use the good, bad, and ugly to help us grow as Christians in our marriage. Seeing through a kingdom lens is looking at everything through the scope of God's word. When the wife allows the Spirit and word of God to open the eyes of her heart, she will not be easily deceived or discouraged, and she will become a partner in spiritual warfare, respecting her husband as unto the Lord.

I've had wives ask me, "What if my husband is not honoring God, and living in rebellion of God's word? Do I have to respect him then?" The simple answer is yes. I take you to 1 Peter 3:1–2:

> Likewise, wives, be subject to your own husbands, so that even if some do not obey the word, they may be won without a word by the conduct of their wives, when they see your respectful and pure conduct.

God will use your obedience to his word, sister, to in your marriage.

The reason you respect your husband is because you are really looking past him to Christ Jesus, to activate the grace of God on him, a flawed man trying to lead and fulfill his role in marriage for God's glory.

What does respect look like to him?

Men, for the most part, are uncomplicated in their desires; thus, they are pretty easy to please when it comes to their emotional and physical needs. Every man is different, but I offer here a list of practical ways for wives to show respect to their husbands. Every item on the list may not be applicable to every marriage, but this is a good starting point.

Before I get to the list, I just need to say, there are factors that could make this challenging if there has been abuse or dysfunctionality in the background of his life. This could look like rejection or abandonment by one or both parents—or verbal, emotional, or physical abuse from family or past relationships. These negative experiences can have lasting effects on the male's psyche if not processed properly. To keep their ego intact, men would usually rather suppress and bury their emotional pain, hoping to keep it hidden from the real world, while they present the facade of control and composure. Unfortunately, these carefully tucked-away emotions are only a trigger away when he feels disrespected or unfairly accused by his wife. For further discussion on this matter, refer back to chapter 2 and the section titled "Personal emotional triggers."

Want versus need. Most men want their wives to be independent, but also to invite them to do things with her because it means more when he is there. Your husband wants a wife who doesn't need him, but asks for him to be in her life because she wants him.

Priorities: Men want to feel that their wife is in tune and connected to their needs. They don't want to compete with other endless tasks on her to-do list. Wives can mistake his frustration as being selfish, not understanding he only wants her to consider him not as a chore but as her man. Husbands like to be romanced and get surprises just as much as wives do; it says to them in the midst of everything going on, "I thought of you. I love you."

Emotional safety. A husband likes to know that his wife won't take advantage of his shortcomings, and will keep his insecurities safe while he's working on them.

A husband wants to know that his wife is supportive of him, even in their challenges, and won't use his challenges as reasons to make him feel like a failure, or that his wife will walk away or abandon him in the relationship. Your husband probably already has come to the realization that marriage challenges his weaknesses, and they can make him feel insecure. He wants you to understand the emotional and psychological strain that comes with being afraid of failing as a husband, yet he cannot always put it into words without sounding like less of a man.

The wife who understands the power of her influence will create a sanctuary for her husband to open up to her and God about his struggles.

Sex. It may be easy to just write men's sexual cravings off as always being horny, but women would be surprised how much of men's desires are actually driven by a need for more intimacy. Of course, men like the physical and visual part of sex, but men also appreciate the real closeness and emotional bonding that comes with sex. What is often misunderstood is that sex with his wife, for the husband, is what recalibrates his heart and mind, connecting his feelings to her renewed. It opens him up to emotional bonding when she presents herself as a lover and a friend.

Affection. Men need intimacy just as women; most men love being married to their wives. Family is important to them, and they love being a dad. Just because they do not always love running errands, or going shopping for groceries and using coupons, it shouldn't disqualify them from expressions of your love. A simple hug, kisses, or surprise from you for no reason—all things that you enjoy receiving—go a long way with husbands too.

Downtime. Sometimes men just need space to process everything going on in their life. It's not isolation, it's not rejecting or avoiding; it is a reflection of all things, just to be alone with their thoughts. It is much appreciated when it is understood without subtle forms of retaliation. When the wife understands this, she can actually nurture it for him, which he will very much appreciate and love her for.

Bathroom freedom. Allow the restroom to be a place of personal activity unless invited. Just because he doesn't have the same bathroom routines that you do doesn't mean something is wrong with him. It is often a place of reading and relaxing, which help him process without interruptions.

The guy pass. This pass is not meant to be the excuses that keep him away from his responsibilities of marriage or the home; it should be a consideration of his need to be socially healthy. Unless he is bankrupting you and not giving back to the love bank, let your husband indulge in his hobbies; allow him to be a man doing man stuff. Encourage him; be his cheerleader on the sideline.

Sex appeal. A husband finds his wife attractive as long as she makes herself attractive for him. Whatever your husband enjoys most about your body, flaunt it for him from time to time.

Conclusion

I know this list is just a glimpse into the world of your husband's thinking, but take note and apply these tips when appropriate.

Reflection questions:

1. Do I respect my husband for who he is?
2. Do I allow room for Jesus to challenge him before I criticize?
3. How can I help him rise above past failures?

CHAPTER 10

Closing the Gaps

The good news that I want to share to anyone who might be in the midst of a struggling marriage, or those who may have concerns about where their marriage is headed right now is that there is hope in Jesus to reconcile and restore your marriage, no matter how much pain you have experienced, or maybe are experiencing right now. If there is a glimpse of hope in your heart to make your marriage work, it can be healed and restored even better than before. I've had the privilege to witness the grace of God in circumstances that should have destroyed a marriage; but because hope would not be surrendered, forgiveness ruled the day. Brokenness and contrition paved the way for redemption and restoration, and God does his best work when things look hopeless.

I don't think God ever determined that sin would destroy the marriage relationship; it's the work of the accuser that makes us feel the need to punish and judge each other when we fall short, or fail in our marriage relationtionship. In the Old Testament, God allowed vindication

THE BRIDGE BETWEEN US
THE BRIDGE BETWEEN US

for wrongdoing, by reciprocating back to the offender what was received from them. An eye for an eye, a life for a life; this was permitted because the law was the standard, and every man was held to the rule of the law. If you failed or broke the law, a penalty had to be paid.

In Christ, we have a different standard called grace. God tells us to not repay evil for evil. Jesus tells us to turn the other cheek. Instead of pointing out the wrong to accuse and judge our spouse, we expose the enemy behind the wrong, so together we can overcome the enemy to restore our spouse in Christ. This is what the Pharisees failed to see with the woman caught in adultery. Jesus is more concerned with restoring her than accusing her, because he was about to pay the price for her sin. He asked her, "Woman, where are your accusers?"

Then he replied, "Neither do I condemn you." What he was communicating in that statement was powerful; "I'll make room for you to repent so you can be redeemed. Now go and sin no more."

> The scribes and the Pharisees brought a woman who had been caught in adultery, and placing her in the midst they said to him, "Teacher, this woman has been caught in the act of adultery. Now in the Law, Moses commanded us to stone such women. So what do you say?" This they said to test him, that they might have some charge to bring against him. Jesus bent down and wrote with his finger on

the ground. And as they continued to
ask him, he stood up and said to them,
"Let him who is without sin among you
be the first to throw a stone at her." And
once more he bent doswn and wrote on
the ground. But when they heard it, they
went away one by one, beginning with the
older ones, and Jesus was left alone with
the woman standing before him. Jesus
stood up and said to her, "Woman, where
are they? Has no one condemned you?"
She said, "No one, Lord." And Jesus said,
"Neither do I condemn you; go, and from
now on sin no more." (John 8:3–11 ESV)

I remember watching several years ago the Christian
music artist Kurt Franklin give his testimony about his
struggle with pornography, as a Christian artist writing and
producing Christian songs. He was a married man serving
God, but plagued with the shame of this dark secret he'd
had in his life since the age of nine years old. He couldn't
take it anymore, so he opened up to his wife about his struggle, and he discovered the gift he had in her. She assured
him that it wasn't his fight alone, but their fight together.
That is the picture of marriage: when one is weak, the other
supports and holds up.

In this final chapter, I want to focus on three things
that will keep the potholes on our bridges fill, and keep us
dancing smoothly over them.

Compassion

This is a sympathetic consciousness of others' distress, together with a desire to alleviate it. It removes contention from any stressful moment when we can see our spouse with eyes of compassion in their plight, whatever their struggle may be. This is not to sound unreasonable at the cost of selfishness or neglect toward either spouse. There are times when intent to harm is absent, but the pain is there nevertheless. The question is, Why should I have compassion for my spouse when I feel hurt by them? Because it keeps the bridge (*open communication*) a safe place to admit unintended wrongdoing in genuine sincerity. It also closes the door to the spirit of resentment, and we are more like Christ when we can see beyond faults to still show compassion.

Couples would benefit if they would learn how to make room for the individuality of their spouse without feeling the need to fix what they don't like about them.

We should consider that Jesus may not be as concerned about that particular area of our spouse as we are; if he is, our gracious behavior will help with the process of change.

> Therefore, as God's chosen people, holy and dearly loved, clothe yourselves with compassion, kindness, humility, gentleness and patience. (Colossians 3:12)

> Be kind and compassionate to one
> another, forgiving each other, just as in
> Christ God forgave you. (Ephesians 4:32)

In compassion, there is no room for irreconcilable expression.

Compliments

These are expressions of esteem, respect, affection, or admiration. Isn't it funny that we can get in the habit of telling each other "I love you," but can go days, weeks, even months without giving each other a genuine compliment? I think this is largely because of uncomfortableness because we have functioned in debtor relationships in our past. I find it hard to receive praise or admiration because I've been made to feel that I need to earn your affection and praise. If you compliment me, I'm in debt to you, and need to earn my way out of your debt. If couples practice esteeming each other whenever they can, it will create a hedge of emotional security in their spouse, which will ward off suspicion and inspire confidence.

As I mentioned in previous chapters, we all need admiration from our spouse to feel confirmed in our marriage. If we practice complimenting more, it would take the sting out of the challenging times in marriage. The magic ratio of criticism is, for every negative comment you make, you need to make five positive comments to make it forgettable. We remember the negative comments longer because they impact our emotional psyche and impact our soul.

Complimenting each other should be a staple in our marriage relationship. So compliment your spouse as often as you have the opportunity.

Cultivation

When we cultivate something, we improve it by labor, care, or study. Listen to me right here. Lazy people should not get married; there is a work to marriage that never stops. People who are not acquainted with death do not make healthy spouses. What I mean is, people who have not cultivated godliness in their life by dying to their flesh do not have a vision for oneness. It is work to remain teachable and changing in the marriage relationship. Why is it that we deceive ourselves by declaring we are growing as Christians, but it is obvious that we are not growing in marriage? Jesus says in the Book of John:

> I tell you the truth, unless a kernel
> of wheat falls to the ground and dies, it
> remains only a single seed. But if it dies, it
> produces many seeds. (John 12:24)

We must be willing to die to unfruitful habits or behavior to cultivate oneness in our marriage. That means anything that competes or conflicts with our spouse, we must be willing to let die, even if it's something that we've tolerated all of our life. I've counseled couples who remain in contention simply because one spouse was unwilling to become amicable for the sake of winning their spouse to their point of view, or allowing themselves to be convinced to their spouse's point of view. Personalities can create extremes in any relationship, but when personality becomes THE thing that makes the relationship struggle, it is time to examine where change is needed. When we make change for our spouse, we communicate to them that they are important to us, and we're willing to die to our flesh to show our love. If couples learn to do this for each other, it would transform their relationship from irreconcilable to inseparable.

Conclusion

Failures will come, offenses will come, but if we can use words that heal instead of words that hurt, we will have an opportunity to partner with God to overcome all obstacles in marriage. So let's close some doors to unwanted invaders, disarm and renounce the hurtful past, and commit to the hopeful future.

Reflection questions:

Below resource is from "Family Life."

References:

Family Life *This article was taken from* Becoming a Woman Who Pleases God, © 2003, by Pat Ennis and Lisa Tatlock. Used by permission of Moody Publishers.
Definition of compassion by Merriam-Webster

Communication

> Good communication is important for all success-ful relationships. When communication breaks down, so do many other aspects of a relationship. The truth is, communication rarely breaks down overnight. It is the subtle eroding away that is oftentimes difficult to see happening. Evaluating your communication and understanding some of your patterns together are a very helpful way to begin assessing the state of your relationship. Respond with *true* or *false* to the following statements. When finished, compare your score to the assessment scale below.

1. We have a least one meaningful conversation per day. *True False*
2. We regularly share our daily routines with one another. *True False*
3. We talk about difficult or challenging issues in a safe and relaxed way. *True False*
4. When my partner calls on the telephone, I always answer. *True False*
5. When we argue, we make efforts to avoid sarcasm or name-calling. *True False*
6. When we have a disagreement, we are able to com-promise or agree to disagree. *True False*
7. Our relationship is not at risk during disagree-ments or confrontations. *True False*

8. Even when we disagree, I feel like my partner has respect for my opinions. *True False*

9. When an argument or discussion gets out of control, we routinely call time-out. *True False*

10. I feel comfortable talking about sexual issues with my partner. *True False*

11. We don't assume we know what one another is thinking. *True False*

12. We don't assume our partner should know what we are thinking. *True False*

13. I feel comfortable talking about difficult issues with my partner. *True False*

14. I regularly try to see my partner's perspective on things. *True False*

15. When we fight or argue, we rarely raise our voices. *True False*

16. I feel I can trust what my partner says to me. *True False*

17. I am satisfied with the level and frequency of our communication. *True False*

18. We never go to bed angry. *True False*

19. The majority of our conversations are stress-free and productive. *True False*

20. When we speak, I feel like my partner is really listening. *True False*

Assessment Score:

ASSESSMENT SCALE

0–8: ON THE EDGE: communication has broken down, likely impacting all areas of your relationship.

9–15: HOLDING STEADY: not bad, but you could make some adjustments to avoid the brink.

16–20: FAR FROM THE EDGE. GREAT job! You're wonderful communicators. Nothing to worry about.

Better communication between partners is always a priority. When you unblock stuck and unhelpful communication patterns, and people have an opportunity to really understand one another, better communication always follows.

ABOUT THE AUTHOR

Dr. Rick D. Merritt's specialties include marital, family, and parenting relationship issues: addictions, change management, depression/anxiety, military, and work-life balance. Over the last twenty-five years, he's gained considerable experience and expertise helping others find emotional relief from the burdens of everyday living, especially issues complicated by self-doubt, self-rejection, and behavioral ruts.

Rick D. Merritt, PhD is founder and president of Heart & Soul Family Counseling Services. Born and raised in Louisiana, Dr. Rick D. Merritt has southern wit and charm, along with a dedicated drive for excellence. He is husband of thirty-eight years to his wife, Judith Merritt, with three children and twelve grandchildren.

He served eight years in the military before resigning to civilian life and devoting himself to full-time ministry in Yuma, Arizona. His pastorate experience began as the associate pastor at his mother church in 1990, which led to his personal calling and ministry three years later as an international evangelist with the Potter's House Ministry.

He is the senior pastor at 180 Faith Ministries in Vista, California, since 1996 reaching the Tri-City and North

County area. The church has local impact on Camp Pendleton and Miramar Naval Base and surrounding community.

He has a PhD in pastoral care and clinical counseling; he is a certified MFT (marriage family therapist), and belongs to the American Academy of Clinical Family Therapists Association, along with other certifications from Light University and the American Association of Christian Counselors in premarital and marital coaching.

Dr. Rick D. Merritt has worked with the Chaplain's Association on military bases to help service members and their families ravaged by years of war. He has partnered and participated in the marriage family and parenting expos held at both at Camp Pendleton and Miramar marine and naval bases.

Dr. Rick D. Merritt is currently putting his experience of over twenty-five years into his private practice Heart & Soul Family Counseling Services in Vista California. He can be contacted at P.O. BOX 2722 Vista, California 92085.

He provides service to couples and families in San Diego, North County, San Bernardino, and Riverside County.

Officiating marriages and family counseling has been a part of Dr. Merritt's ministry for over twenty-five years. He has also had the privilege of marrying the VIP couple LeBron and Savannah James in 2013, at the Grand Del Mar hotel in San Diego, California.